PREOCCUPATIONS

DATE DUE

SEAMUS HEANEY

Preoccupations

SELECTED PROSE
1968–1978

The Noonday Press
Farrar, Straus and Giroux
New York

Copyright © 1980 by Seamus Heaney
All rights reserved
This collection first published in 1980 by Faber and Faber Limited
First American printing, 1980
Printed in the United States of America

Library of Congress Cataloging in Publication Data
Heaney, Seamus.
Preoccupations.
I. Title.
PR6058.E2P7   1980   821'.009   80-21271

Fourth printing, 1990

for Seamus Deane and Thomas Flanagan

Acknowledgements

The author and publisher would like to acknowledge the following: BBC Radio, Carcanet Press, *Critical Inquiry*, *Education Times*, the *Guardian*, *Hibernia*, *Honest Ulsterman*, the *Irish Times*, the *Listener*, Penguin Books, *Proceedings of the British Academy*, Radio Telefís Eireann, *Threshold* and *The Times Literary Supplement*.

Acknowledgements are also due to André Deutsch Ltd for permission to quote from *Mercian Hymns* (1975) by Geoffrey Hill; and to Mrs Katherine B. Kavanagh and Martin Brian & O'Keeffe Ltd for permission to quote from Patrick Kavanagh's poems.

Foreword

Except for a couple of reviews and a *Listener* article of 1971, all of the pieces printed here were written during or since 1972. Yet long before that critical year the sediment out of which many of them spring had been gathering, especially in Belfast in the mid-sixties, when a group of us who had just started to write used to talk poetry day after day with an intensity and a prejudice that cannot but have left a mark on all of us. Then at Easter in 1972 I decided to resign from my entirely agreeable job in the English Department of Queen's University, and that summer I moved with my family to Glanmore in Co. Wicklow, determined to put the practice of poetry more deliberately at the centre of my life. It was a kind of test.

All that I really knew about the art was derived from whatever poetry I had written, and from those poets who had helped me to write it. I had a half-clarified desire to come to poetic terms with myself by considering the example of others, and to try to bring into focus the little I knew. So when my freelance activities inevitably led to lecturing and reviewing, the focusing began on that occasional basis. But I hope it is clear that the essays selected here are held together by searches for answers to central preoccupying questions: how should a poet properly live and write? What is his relationship to be to his own voice, his own place, his literary heritage and his contemporary world?

The longer pieces were written to be delivered from the podium so now and again that lecturing note creeps in. And if there is sometimes a strait-laced quality about the writing, that too is all part of 'the makings of a music', the slightly constricted utterance of somebody who underwent his academic rite of passage when practical criticism held great sway in the academy. Nevertheless, I am grateful for that discipline: as Finn McCool said in his time, the best music in the world is the music of what happens.

We go on, of course, to blunder after the music of what might happen, a quest which requires confidants and mentors, and this book is a response to some who came to my assistance. A number of the essays are obviously a matter of 'breaking bread with the dead', an activity which W. H. Auden judged essential to the life of poetry. Others are just as clearly engagements with the achievements of the living; and others still are inspections of myself, although, as Patrick Kavanagh insisted, the self is interesting only as an example.

Many people who are not mentioned in these pages have left their mark upon them: among many excellent teachers, Sean B. O'Kelly at St. Columb's College and Laurence Lerner at Queen's, both of whom quickened my love of poetry and, for better or worse, helped to start me writing about it; Michael McLaverty, who lent me Patrick Kavanagh's *A Soul for Sale* late in 1962; Edna Longley, whose comprehension of Edward Thomas extended into a reading of the contemporary English poets discussed here along similar lines; Michael Allen, the reader over my shoulder; and Helen Vendler, who encouraged me to trust my critical capacities even after she had read some of these chapters in manuscript. To the friends named on the dedication page I owe a special debt of gratitude; over the years, their conversation, their writings and their formal lectures have given me food for the thought that nurtured much of what follows. Indeed in one or two places it appears entirely undigested.

Since I have always needed to be goaded into this kind of work, I am in more than the usual debt to the editors who commissioned and patiently awaited the different articles and reviews, and to the sponsors of the lectures. And since nobody except my wife Marie has been privy to the turbulence in the house as I kicked against these goads, I have to thank her more than anybody for putting up with and encouraging me during the whole uncertain business.

Contents

At the enquiry which preceded the granting of a patent to the Abbey Theatre I was asked if *Cathleen ni Houlihan* was not written to affect opinion. Certainly it was not. I had a dream one night which gave me a story, and I had certain emotions about this country, and I gave those emotions expression for my own pleasure. If I had written to convince others I would have asked myself, not 'Is that exactly what I think and feel?' but 'How would that strike so-and-so? How will they think and feel when they have read it?' And all would be oratorical and insincere. If we understand our own minds, and the things that are striving to utter themselves through our minds, we move others, not because we have understood or thought about those others, but because all life has the same root. Coventry Patmore has said, 'The end of art is peace,' and the following of art is little different from the following of religion in the intense preoccupation it demands.

W. B. YEATS, 'Samhain: 1905', in *Explorations*

I

Mossbawn

1. *Omphalos*

I would begin with the Greek word, *omphalos*, meaning the navel, and hence the stone that marked the centre of the world, and repeat it, *omphalos, omphalos, omphalos*, until its blunt and falling music becomes the music of somebody pumping water at the pump outside our back door. It is Co. Derry in the early 1940s. The American bombers groan towards the aerodrome at Toomebridge, the American troops manoeuvre in the fields along the road, but all of that great historical action does not disturb the rhythms of the yard. There the pump stands, a slender, iron idol, snouted, helmeted, dressed down with a sweeping handle, painted a dark green and set on a concrete plinth, marking the centre of another world. Five households drew water from it. Women came and went, came rattling between empty enamel buckets, went evenly away, weighed down by silent water. The horses came home to it in those first lengthening evenings of spring, and in a single draught emptied one bucket and then another as the man pumped and pumped, the plunger slugging up and down, *omphalos, omphalos, omphalos*.

I do not know what age I was when I got lost in the pea-drills in a field behind the house, but it is a half-dream to me, and I've heard about it so often that I may even be imagining it. Yet, by now, I have imagined it so long and so often that I know what it was like: a green web, a caul of veined light, a tangle of rods and pods, stalks and tendrils, full of assuaging earth and leaf smell, a sunlit lair. I'm sitting as if just wakened from a winter sleep and gradually become aware of voices, coming closer, calling my name, and for no reason at all I have begun to weep.

All children want to crouch in their secret nests. I loved the

17

fork of a beech tree at the head of our lane, the close thicket of a boxwood hedge in the front of the house, the soft, collapsing pile of hay in a back corner of the byre; but especially I spent time in the throat of an old willow tree at the end of the farmyard. It was a hollow tree, with gnarled, spreading roots, a soft, perishing bark and a pithy inside. Its mouth was like the fat and solid opening in a horse's collar, and, once you squeezed in through it, you were at the heart of a different life, looking out on the familiar yard as if it were suddenly behind a pane of strangeness. Above your head, the living tree flourished and breathed, you shouldered the slightly vibrant bole, and if you put your forehead to the rough pith you felt the whole lithe and whispering crown of willow moving in the sky above you. In that tight cleft, you sensed the embrace of light and branches, you were a little Atlas shouldering it all, a little Cerunnos pivoting a world of antlers.

The world grew. Mossbawn, the first place, widened. There was what we called the Sandy Loaning, a sanded pathway between old hedges leading in off the road, first among fields and then through a small bog, to a remote farmhouse. It was a silky, fragrant world there, and for the first few hundred yards you were safe enough. The sides of the lane were banks of earth topped with broom and ferns, quilted with moss and primroses. Behind the broom, in the rich grass, cattle munched reassuringly. Rabbits occasionally broke cover and ran ahead of you in a flurry of dry sand. There were wrens and goldfinches. But, gradually, those lush and definite fields gave way to scraggy marshland. Birch trees stood up to their pale shins in swamps. The ferns thickened above you. Scuffles in old leaves made you nervous and you dared yourself always to pass the badger's set, a wound of fresh mould in an overgrown ditch where the old brock had gone to earth. Around that badger's hole, there hung a field of dangerous force. This was the realm of bogeys. We'd heard about a mystery man who haunted the fringes of the bog here, we talked about mankeepers and moss-cheepers, creatures uncatalogued by any naturalist, but none the less real for that. What was a mosscheeper, anyway, if not the soft, malicious sound the word itself made, a siren of collapsing sibilants coaxing you out towards bog pools lidded with innocent grass, quicksands and quagmires? They were all there and spreading out over a low, birch-screened apron of land towards the shores of Lough Beg.

That was the moss, forbidden ground. Two families lived at the heart of it, and a recluse, called Tom Tipping, whom we never saw, but in the morning on the road to school we watched his smoke rising from a clump of trees, and spoke his name between us until it was synonymous with mystery man, with unexpected scuttlings in the hedge, with footsteps slushing through long grass.

To this day, green, wet corners, flooded wastes, soft rushy bottoms, any place with the invitation of watery ground and tundra vegetation, even glimpsed from a car or a train, possess an immediate and deeply peaceful attraction. It is as if I am betrothed to them, and I believe my betrothal happened one summer evening, thirty years ago, when another boy and myself stripped to the white country skin and bathed in a moss-hole, treading the liver-thick mud, unsettling a smoky muck off the bottom and coming out smeared and weedy and darkened. We dressed again and went home in our wet clothes, smelling of the ground and the standing pool, somehow initiated.

Beyond the moss spread the narrow reaches of Lough Beg, and in the centre of Lough Beg lay Church Island, a spire rising out of its yew trees, a local mecca. St. Patrick, they said, had fasted and prayed there fifteen hundred years before. The old graveyard was shoulder-high with meadowsweet and cow parsley, overhung with thick, unmolested yew trees and, somehow, those yews fetched me away to Agincourt and Crécy, where the English archers' bows, I knew, were made of yew also. All I could ever manage for my bows were tapering shoots of ash or willow from a hedge along the stackyard, but even so, to have cut a bough from that silent compound on Church Island would have been a violation too treacherous to contemplate.

If Lough Beg marked one limit of the imagination's nesting ground, Slieve Gallon marked another. Slieve Gallon is a small mountain that lies in the opposite direction, taking the eye out over grazing and ploughed ground and the distant woods of Moyola Park, out over Grove Hill and Back Park and Castledawson. This side of the country was the peopled, communal side, the land of haycock and corn-stook, of fence and gate, milk-cans at the end of lanes and auction notices on gate pillars. Dogs barked from farm to farm. Sheds gaped at the roadside, bulging with fodder. Behind and across it went the railway, and the noise that hangs over it constantly is the heavy shunting of an engine at Castledawson station.

I have a sense of air, of lift and light, when this comes back to me. Light dancing off the shallows of the Moyola River, shifting in eddies on the glaucous whirlpool. Light changing on the mountain itself, that stood like a barometer of moods, now blue and hazy, now green and close up. Light above the spire, away at Magherafelt. Light frothing among the bluebells on Grove Hill. And the lift of the air is resonant, too, with vigorous musics. A summer evening carries the fervent and melancholy strain of hymn-singing from a gospel hall among the fields, and the hawthorn blooms and the soft, white patens of the elder-flower hang dolorous in the hedges. Or the rattle of Orange drums from Aughrim Hill sets the heart alert and watchful as a hare.

For if this was the country of community, it was also the realm of division. Like the rabbit pads that loop across grazing, and tunnel the soft growths under ripening corn, the lines of sectarian antagonism and affiliation followed the boundaries of the land. In the names of its fields and townlands, in their mixture of Scots and Irish and English etymologies, this side of the country was redolent of the histories of its owners. Broagh, The Long Rigs, Bell's Hill; Brian's Field, the Round Meadow, the Demesne; each name was a kind of love made to each acre. And saying the names like this distances the places, turns them into what Wordsworth once called a prospect of the mind. They lie deep, like some script indelibly written into the nervous system.

I always remember the pleasure I had in digging the black earth in our garden and finding, a foot below the surface, a pale seam of sand. I remember, too, men coming to sink the shaft of the pump and digging through that seam of sand down into the bronze riches of the gravel, that soon began to puddle with the spring water. That pump marked an original descent into earth, sand, gravel, water. It centred and staked the imagination, made its foundation the foundation of the *omphalos* itself. So I find it altogether appropriate that an old superstition ratifies this hankering for the underground side of things. It is a superstition associated with the Heaney name. In Gaelic times, the family were involved with ecclesiastical affairs in the diocese of Derry, and had some kind of rights to the stewardship of a monastic site at Banagher in the north of the county. There is a St. Muredach O'Heney associated with the old church at Banagher; and there is also a belief that sand lifted from the ground at Banagher has beneficent, even magical, properties, if it is lifted from the site by one of the Heaney family name. Throw sand that a Heaney has lifted after a man going into court, and he will win his case. Throw it after your team as they go out on the pitch, and they will win the game.

BBC Radio 4, 1978

2. Reading

When I was learning to read, towards the end of 1945, the most important books in the house were the ration books—the pink clothes coupons and the green 'points' for sweets and groceries. There wasn't much reading done apart from the deaths column of the *Irish Weekly* and the auctions page of the *Northern Constitution*. 'I am instructed by the representatives of the late John James Halferty, Drumanee . . .' My father lay on the sofa and rehearsed the acres, roods and perches of arable and meadow land in a formal tone and with a certain enlargement of the spirit.

On a shelf, behind a screen and too high to be reached anyhow, there were four or five mouldering volumes that may have belonged to my Aunt Susan from her days in Orange's Academy, but they remained closed books to me. The first glimpse I have of myself reading on my own is one of those orphaned memories, a moment without context that will always stay with me. It is a book from the school library—a padlocked box that was opened more or less as a favour—involving explorers in cork helmets and 'savages', with illustrations of war canoes on a jungle river. The oil lamp is lit and a neighbour called Hugh Bates is interrupting me. 'Boys but this Seamus fellow is a great scholar. What book are you in now, son?' And my father is likely wringing what he can from the moment with 'He's as bad as Pat McGuckin this minute.' Pat McGuckin was a notorious bachelor farmer—a cousin of ours—who was said to burn his scone like King Alfred every time he lifted a book. Years later, when *Death of a Naturalist* was published, the greatest commendation at home was 'Lord knows Pat would fairly have enjoyed this.'

Of course, there were always religious magazines like the *Far East* and the *Messenger*—Pudsy Ryan in the children's corner of the former was the grown-ups' idea of a side-splitting turn, but even then I found his mis-spellings a bit heavy-handed. Far better were the technicolour splendours of Korky the Cat and Big Eggo in the *Dandy* and *Beano*. The front pages of these comics opened like magic casements on Desperate Dan, Lord Snooty, Hungry Horace, Keyhole Kate, Julius Sneezer and Jimmy and his Magic Patch and probably constituted my first sense of the invitations of fiction. They were passed round at school, usually fairly tattered, but every now and again my mother brought a new one from Castledawson, without a fold in it, its primary colours blazing with excitements to come. Occasionally, also, an American comic—all colour from beginning to end—arrived from the American airbase nearby, with Li'l Abner, Ferdinand and Blondie speaking a language that even Pat McGuckin did not know.

There was a resistance to buying new comics in our house, not out of any educational nicety, but because of a combination of two attitudes: that they were a catch-penny and that somehow they were the thin end of the wedge, that if you let them into the house the next step was the *Empire News*, *Thompson's Weekly*, *Tit-Bits* and the *News of the World*. Nevertheless, I ended up persuading my mother to place a regular order for the *Champion*, a higher-class comic altogether, featuring a Biggles-rides-again figure called Rockfist Rogan and Ginger Nutt ('the boy who takes the *bis-cake*', in South Derry parlance) and Colwyn Dane, the sleuth. With the *Champion* I entered the barter market for the *Rover*, the *Hotspur*, the *Wizard* and any other pulp the presses of old England could deliver. I skimmed through all those 'ain'ts' and 'cors' and 'yoicks' and 'blimeys', and skimmed away contented.

So what chance had Kitty the Hare against all that? *Our Boys* appeared regularly, a cultural antidote with official home backing, healthy as a Christian Brother on a winter morning, the first step towards *Ireland's Own*. Cultural debilitations! I preferred the japes of Ginger Nutt, the wheezes of Smith of the Lower Fourth, the swish of gowns, the mortar-board and the head's study to the homely toils of Murphy among the birettas. It would take Joyce's *Portrait of the Artist as a Young Man* and Kavanagh's *The Great Hunger* to get over that surrender.

My first literary *frisson*, however, came on home ground. There was an Irish history lesson at school which was in reality a reading of myths and legends. A textbook with large type and heavy Celticized illustrations dealt with the matter of Ireland from the Tuatha De Danaan to the Norman Invasion. I can still see Brian Boru with his sword held like a cross reviewing the troops at Clontarf. But the real imaginative mark was made with a story of the Dagda, a dream of harp music and light, confronting and defeating Balor of the Evil Eye on the dark fortress of Tory Island. Cuchullain and Ferdia also sank deep, those images of wounds bathed on the green rushes and armour clattering in the ford.

Yet all of that yielded to the melodrama of Blind Pew and Billy Bones, Long John and Ben Gunn. *Treasure Island* we read at school also and it was a prelude to the first book I remember owning and cherishing: there it was on the table one Christmas morning, Robert Louis Stevenson's *Kidnapped*. I was a Jacobite for life after that day. Instinctively I knew that the world of the penal rock and the redcoats—that oleograph to the faith of our fathers—was implicit in the scenery of that story. To this day, my heart lifts to the first sentence of it: 'I will begin the story of my adventures with a certain morning in the month of June, the year of grace 1751, when I took the key for the last time out of the door of my father's house. . . .'

As a boarder at St. Columb's College I did the Maurice Walsh circuit—*Blackcock's Feather* remains with me as an atmosphere, a sense of bogs and woods—but again it was a course book that stuck its imagery deepest. When I read in *Lorna Doone* how John Ridd stripped the muscle off Carver Doone's arm like a string of pith off an orange I was well on the road to epiphanies. Not that I didn't stray into the imperial realms of Biggles or the baloney of the William stories. But it is only those books with a touch of poetry in them that I can remember—

all coming to a head when, in my last summer holiday from school, I sat up all night to finish Thomas Hardy's *Return of the Native*.

I missed Pooh Bear. I can't remember owning a selection of Grimm or Andersen. I read *Alice in Wonderland* at the university. But what odds? Didn't Vinny Hunter keep me in wonderland with his stories of Tarzan:

> 'When he jumps down off a tree
> Tarzan shakes the world.'
> So Vinny Hunter would tell me
> On the road to the school.

> I had forgotten for years
> Words so seismic and plain
> That would come like rocked waters,
> Possible again.

Education Times, 1973

3. Rhymes

A few months ago I remembered a rhyme that we used to chant on the way to school. I know now that it is about initiation but as I trailed along the Lagan's Road on my way to Anahorish School it was something that was good for a laugh:

> 'Are your praties dry
> And are they fit for digging?'
> 'Put in your spade and try,'
> Says Dirty-Faced McGuigan.

I suppose I must have been about eight or nine years old when those lines stuck in my memory. They constitute a kind of poetry, not very respectable perhaps, but very much alive on the lips of that group of schoolboys, or 'scholars', as the older people were inclined to call us. McGuigan was probably related to a stern old character called Ned McGuigan who travelled the roads with a menacing blackthorn stick. He came from a district called Ballymacquigan—The Quigan, for short—and he turned up in another rhyme:

Neddy McGuigan,
He pissed in the Quigan;
The Quigan was hot
So he pissed in the pot;
The pot was too high
So he pissed in the sky;
Hell to your soul, Neddy McGuigan,
For pissing so high.

And there were other chants, scurrilous and sectarian, that we used to fling at one another:

Up the long ladder and down the short rope
To hell with King Billy and God bless the Pope.

To which the answer was:

Up with King William and down with the Pope

Splitter splatter holy water
Scatter the Paypishes every one
If that won't do
We'll cut them in two
And give them a touch of the⁻
Red, white and blue.

To which the answer was:

Red, white and blue
Should be torn up in two
And sent to the devil
At half-past two.
Green, white and yellow
Is a decent fellow.

Another one which was completely nonsensical still pleases me:

One fine October's morning September last July
The moon lay thick upon the ground, the mud shone in the sky.
I stepped into a tramcar to take me across the sea,
I asked the conductor to punch my ticket and he punched my eye
    for me.

I fell in love with an Irish girl, she sang me an Irish dance,
She lived in Tipperary, just a few miles out of France.
The house it was a round one, the front was at the back,
It stood alone between two more and it was whitewashed black.

We weren't forced to get these lines by heart. They just seemed to spring in our mind and trip off the tongue spontaneously so that our parents would say 'If it was your prayers, you wouldn't learn them as fast.'

There were other poems, of course, that we were forced to learn by heart. I am amazed to realize that at the age of eleven I was spouting great passages of Byron and Keats by rote until the zinc roof of the Nissen hut that served for our schoolhouse (the previous school had been cleared during the war to make room for an aerodrome) rang to the half-understood magnificence of:

> There was a sound of revelry by night
> And Belgium's capital had gathered then
> Her beauty and her chivalry, and bright
> The lamps shone o'er fair women and brave men.
> A thousand hearts beat happily; and when
> The music rose with its voluptuous swell ...

I also knew the whole of Keats's ode 'To Autumn' but the only line that was luminous then was 'To bend with apples the mossed cottage trees', because my uncle had a small orchard where the old apple trees were sleeved in a soft green moss. And I had a vague satisfaction from 'the small gnats mourn/Among the river sallows', which would have been complete if it had been 'midges' mourning among the 'sallies'.

The literary language, the civilized utterance from the classic canon of English poetry, was a kind of force-feeding. It did not delight us by reflecting our experience; it did not re-echo our own speech in formal and surprising arrangements. Poetry lessons, in fact, were rather like catechism lessons: official inculcations of hallowed formulae that were somehow expected to stand us in good stead in the adult life that stretched out ahead. Both lessons did indeed introduce us to the gorgeousness of the polysyllable, and as far as we were concerned there was little to choose between the music with 'its voluptuous swell' and the 'solemnization of marriage within forbidden degrees of consanguinity'. In each case we were overawed by the dimensions of the sound.

There was a third category of verse which I encountered at this time, halfway between the roadside rhymes and the school poetry (or 'poertry'): a form known to us as 'the recitation'.

When relations visited or a children's party was held at home, I would be called upon to recite. Sometimes it would be an Irish patriotic ballad:

> At length, brave Michael Dwyer, you and your trusty men
> Were hunted o'er the mountain and tracked into the glen.
> Sleep not, but watch and listen, keep ready blade and ball,
> For the soldiers know you hide this night in the Glen of Wild Imall.

Sometimes, a western narrative by Robert Service:

> A bunch of the boys were whooping it up in the Malamute Saloon.
> The kid that handles the music-box was hitting a ragtime tune.
> Back of the bar at a solo game sat Dangerous Dan McGrew
> And watching his luck was his light o'love, the lady that's known as
>   Lou.

While this kind of stuff did not possess the lure of forbidden words like 'piss' and 'hell to your soul', it was not encumbered by the solemn incomprehensibility of Byron and Keats. It gave verse, however humble, a place in the life of the home, made it one of the ordinary rituals of life.

Geoffrey Summerfield (ed.), *Worlds*, Penguin, 1974

Belfast

1. The Group

'If a coathanger knocked in a wardrobe/That was a great event'—Derek Mahon's evocation of the unfulfilled expectancy of an old man living in Belfast could be extended to the young men around Queen's in the late fifties and early sixties. A lot of people of a generally literary bent were islanded about the place but they in no way constituted an archipelago. There was Denis Tuohy, Don Carleton, David Farrell, Stewart Parker, Ian Hill, Seamus Deane, John Hamilton, myself and many another, all dabbling. I don't think many of us had a sense of contemporary poetry—Dylan Thomas's records were as near as we seemed to get to the living thing. Laurence Lerner was in the English Department and produced a collection called *Domestic Interiors* but it was somehow remote, none of our business. And as for Philip Larkin, who had just left, I graduated without hearing his name, from student or lecturer. Michael McLaverty was teaching in town, but we never saw him; Roy McFadden had drawn the blinds on *Rann*, John Hewitt was in Coventry. That older generation were perhaps names to us but not voices. *Gorgon* and *Q*, the university literary magazines, were hand-to-mouth affairs, with no real excitement, audience or clique attaching to them. Mary O'Malley, John Boyd, Sam Hanna Bell, Joseph Tomelty and others were at work but again, they were beyond us. We stood or hung or sleepwalked between notions of writing that we had gleaned from English courses and the living reality of writers from our own place whom we did not know, in person or in print.

Those of us who stayed around saw that state of affairs changed by the mid-sixties and one of the strongest agents of change was Philip Hobsbaum. When Hobsbaum arrived in

Belfast, he moved disparate elements into a single action. He emanated energy, generosity, belief in the community, trust in the parochial, the inept, the unprinted. He was impatient, dogmatic, relentlessly literary: yet he was patient with those he trusted, unpredictably susceptible to a wide variety of poems and personalities and urgent that the social and political exacerbations of our place should disrupt the decorums of literature. If he drove some people mad with his absolutes and hurt others with his overbearing, he confirmed as many with his enthusiasms. He and his wife Hannah kept open house for poetry and I remember his hospitality and encouragement with the special gratitude we reserve for those who have led us towards confidence in ourselves.

I remember especially the first meeting of the group. Stewart Parker read his poems and was the first—and last—writer to stand up as he did so. That ritual of rising up to enounce, that initial formal ratification of the voice, seems emblematic in retrospect. What happened Monday night after Monday night in the Hobsbaum's flat in Fitzwilliam Street somehow ratified the activity of writing for all of us who shared it. Perhaps not everybody needed it ratified—Michael Longley and James Simmons, for example, had been in the swim before they landed—but all of us were part of it in the end. What Hobsbaum achieved, whether people like it or not, was to give a generation a sense of themselves, in two ways: it allowed us to get to grips with one another within the group, to move from critical comment to creative friendship at our own pace, and it allowed a small public to think of us as The Group, a single, even singular phenomenon. There was his introduction of a number of us to 'The Arts in Ulster', produced by John Boyd. There was an article in the *Telegraph*. There was Mary Holland scooping it all for the *Observer* when she arrived to cover the Festival in 1965. It's easy to be blasé about all that now, for now, of course, we're genuine parochials. Then we were craven provincials. Hobsbaum contributed much to that crucial transformation.

When the Hobsbaums left, we missed the regular coffee and biscuits, the irregular booze, the boisterous literary legislation. One act of the drama had closed down. When the second act opened in my own house, after interludes in the back room of the English Department and the upper room of a pub, some of the old characters had departed, to London, Portrush, Holywood, wherever, and a crowd of gifted boy actors were in the wings to claim the stage. But by then the curtain was about to rise on the larger drama of our politics and the writers were to find themselves in a play within the play.

Honest Ulsterman, 1978

2. Christmas, 1971

People keep asking what it's like to be living in Belfast and I've found myself saying that things aren't too bad in our part of the town: a throwaway consolation meaning that we don't expect to be caught in crossfire if we step into the street. It's a shorthand that evades unravelling the weary twisted emotions that are rolled like a ball of hooks and sinkers in the heart. I am fatigued by a continuous adjudication between agony and injustice, swung at one moment by the long tail of race and resentment, at another by the more acceptable feelings of pity and terror. We live in the sickly light of TV screens, with a pane of selfishness between ourselves and the suffering. We survive explosions and funerals and live on among the families of the victims, those blown apart and those in cells apart.

And we have to live with the Army. This morning I was stopped on the Falls Road and marched to the nearest police barracks, with my three-year-old son, because my car tax was out of date. My protests grew limp when the officer in charge said: 'Look, either you go to the police up the road or we take you now to Holywood'—their own ground. It hasn't been named martial law but that's what it feels like. Everywhere soldiers with cocked guns are watching you—that's what they're here for—on the streets, at the corners of streets, from doorways, over the puddles on demolished sites. At night, jeeps and armoured cars groan past without lights; or road-blocks are thrown up, and once again it's delays measured in hours, searches and signings among the guns and torches. As you drive away, you bump over ramps that are specially designed to wreck you at speed and maybe get a glimpse of a couple of youths with hands on their heads being frisked on the far side of the road.

Just routine. Meanwhile up in the troubled estates street-lights are gone, accommodating all the better the night-sights of sniper and marksman.

If it is not army blocks, it is vigilantes. They are very efficiently organized, with barricades of new wood and watchmen's huts and tea rotas, protecting the territories. If I go round the corner at ten o'clock to the cigarette machine or the chip shop, there are the gentlemen with flashlights, of mature years and determined mien, who will want to know my business. How far they are in agreement with the sentiments blazoned on the wall at the far end of the street I have not yet enquired. But 'Keep Ulster Protestant' and 'Keep Blacks and Fenians out of Ulster' are there to remind me that there are attitudes around here other than defensive ones. All those sentry boxes where tea and consultation are taken through the small hours add up to yet another slogan: 'Six into Twenty-Six won't go.' I walk back—'Good-night now, sir'—past a bank that was blown up a couple of months ago and a car showroom that went three weeks ago. Nobody was killed. Most of the windows between the sites are boarded up still. Things aren't too bad in our part.

There are few enough people on the roads at night. Fear has begun to tingle through the place. Who's to know the next target on the Provisional list? Who's to know the reprisals won't strike where you are? The bars are quieter. If you're carrying a parcel you make sure it's close to you in case it's suspected of being about to detonate. In the Queen's University staff common-room, recently, a bomb-disposal squad had defused a bundle of books before the owner had quite finished his drink in the room next door. Yet when you think of the corpses in the rubble of McGurk's Bar such caution is far from risible.

Then there are the perils of the department stores. Last Saturday a bomb scare just pipped me before I had my socks and pyjamas paid for in Marks and Spencer, although there were four people on the Shankill Road who got no warning. A security man cornered my wife in Robinson and Cleaver—not surprisingly, when she thought of it afterwards. She had a timing device, even though it was just an old clock from an auction, lying in the bottom of her shopping bag. A few days previously someone else's timing device had given her a scare when an office block in University Road exploded just as she got out of range.

There are hardly any fairy lights, or Christmas trees, and in many cases there will be no Christmas cards. This latter is the result of a request by the organizers of the civil disobedience campaign, in order that revenue to the Post Office may be cut as much as possible over the joyous season. If people must send cards, then they are asked to get the anti-internment cards which are being produced by the People's Democracy and the Ardoyne Relief Committee to support, among others, the dependants of the internees in Long Kesh camp. Which must, incidentally, be literally the brightest spot in Ulster. When you pass it on the motorway after dark, it is squared off in neon, bright as an airport. An inflammation on the black countryside. Another of our military decorations.

The seasonal appeals will be made again to all men of goodwill, but goodwill for its proper exercise depends upon an achieved self-respect. For some people in this community, the exercise of goodwill towards the dominant caste has been hampered by the psychological hoops they have been made to jump and by the actual circumstances of their lives within the state, British and all as it may have been. A little goodwill in the Establishment here towards the notion of being Irish would take some of the twists out of the minority. Even at this time it is difficult to extend full sympathy to the predicament of that million among us who would ask the other half-million to exalt themselves by being humbled. You see, I have heard a completely unbigoted and humane friend searching for words to cope with his abhorrence of the Provisionals and hitting on the *mot juste* quite unconsciously: 'These ... these ... Irish.'

Instead of the Christmas tree, which will be deliberately absent from many homes, people will put the traditional candle in the window. I am reminded of Louis MacNeice, 'born to the Anglican order, banned for ever from the candles of the Irish poor'; and of W. R. Rodgers, whose *Collected Poems* have appeared in time for Christmas; and of John Hewitt, that Ulsterman of Planter stock whose poetry over the years has been an exploration of the Ulster Protestant consciousness. All three men were born to a sense of 'two nations' and part of their imaginative effort was a solving of their feelings towards

32

Ireland, a new answer to the question that Macmorris asked
Fluellen in the Globe Theatre almost four hundred years ago:
'What is my nation?' As Northern Protestants, they each in
different ways explored their relationship to the old sow that
eats her farrow. They did not hold apart and claim kin with a
different litter. Although, in fact, I have never seen farrow
eaten by a sow in my life: what usually happens is that the young
pigs eat one another's ears.

Last Sunday, at an interdenominational carol service in the
university, I had to read from Martin Luther King's famous 'I
have a dream' speech. 'I have a dream that one day this nation
will rise up and live out the full meaning of its creed'—and on
that day all men would be able to realize fully the implications of
the old spiritual, 'Free at last, free at last, Great God Almighty,
we are free at last.' But, as against the natural hopeful rhythms
of that vision, I remembered a dream that I'd had last year in
California. I was shaving at the mirror of the bathroom when I
glimpsed in the mirror a wounded man falling towards me with
his bloodied hands lifted to tear at me or to implore.

It used to be that you could predict the aftermath of Christmas: 'How did your Christmas go?' 'Oh quiet, very quiet.'
There isn't much predictable now, except that the sirens will
blare out the old and blare in nothing very new. In some parts of
the country they will have killed the wren on St. Stephen's Day.
In some houses they will still be hoping for a first-footer to bring
a change of luck.

Listener, 1971

3. 1972

Two quotations keep going through my mind these days, both
from Shakespeare:

> How with this rage shall beauty hold a plea
> Whose action is no stronger than a flower?

and then these lines from *Timon of Athens* where a poet talks
about the process of writing, lines that have become a touchstone for me:

> Our poesy is as a gum which oozes
> From whence tis nourished.

On the one hand, poetry is secret and natural, on the other hand it must make its way in a world that is public and brutal. Here the explosions literally rattle your window day and night, lives are shattered blandly or terribly, innocent men have been officially beaten and humiliated in internment camps—destructive elements of all kinds, which are even perhaps deeply exhilarating, are in the air.

At one minute you are drawn towards the old vortex of racial and religious instinct, at another time you seek the mean of humane love and reason. Yet is your *raison d'être* not involved with marks on paper? As Patrick Kavanagh said, a man dabbles in verses and finds they are his life.

You have to be true to your own sensibility, for the faking of feelings is a sin against the imagination. Poetry is out of the quarrel with ourselves and the quarrel with others is rhetoric. It would wrench the rhythms of my writing procedures to start squaring up to contemporary events with more will than ways to deal with them. I have always listened for poems, they come sometimes like bodies come out of a bog, almost complete, seeming to have been laid down a long time ago, surfacing with a touch of mystery. They certainly involve craft and determination, but chance and instinct have a role in the thing too. I think the process is a kind of somnambulist encounter between masculine will and intelligence and feminine clusters of image and emotion.

I suppose the feminine element for me involves the matter of Ireland, and the masculine strain is drawn from the involvement with English literature. I speak and write in English, but do not altogether share the preoccupations and perspectives of an Englishman. I teach English literature, I publish in London, but the English tradition is not ultimately home. I live off another hump as well.

Two Elizabethan poets enforce this realization. Edmund Spenser's view of the state of Ireland, among other things, puts me at a distance from him. From his castle in Cork he watched the effects of a campaign designed to settle the Irish question. 'Out of every corner of the woods and glens they came creeping forth upon their hands, for their legs could not carry them; they looked like anatomies of death, they spake like ghosts crying out of their graves.' At that point I feel closer to the natives, the

34

geniuses of the place. And a little after that, Sir John Davies, that silver poet of the sixteenth century, arrived in Ireland as Queen Elizabeth's Attorney-General with special responsibility for the Plantation of Ulster, playing a forward-looking colon to my backward-looking colonisé.

Obviously, these incidental facts do not interfere with my responses to their poetry. One half of one's sensibility is in a cast of mind that comes from belonging to a place, an ancestry, a history, a culture, whatever one wants to call it. But consciousness and quarrels with the self are the result of what Lawrence called 'the voices of my education'.

Those voices pull in two directions, back through the political and cultural traumas of Ireland, and out towards the urgencies and experience of the world beyond it. At school I studied the Gaelic literature of Ireland as well as the literature of England, and since then I have maintained a notion of myself as Irish in a province that insists that it is British. Lately I realized that these complex pieties and dilemmas were implicit in the very terrain where I was born.

Our farm was called Mossbawn. *Moss*, a Scots word probably carried to Ulster by the Planters, and *bawn*, the name the English colonists gave to their fortified farmhouses. Mossbawn, the planter's house on the bog. Yet in spite of this Ordnance Survey spelling, we pronounced it Moss bann, and *bán* is the Gaelic word for white. So might not the thing mean the white moss, the moss of bog-cotton? In the syllables of my home I see a metaphor of the split culture of Ulster.

Mossbawn lies between the villages of Castledawson and Toome. I was symbolically placed between the marks of English influence and the lure of the native experience, between 'the demesne' and 'the bog'. The demesne was Moyola Park, an estate now occupied by Lord Moyola, formerly Major James Chichester-Clark, ex-Unionist Prime Minister of Northern Ireland. The bog was a wide low apron of swamp on the west bank of the River Bann, where hoards of flints and fishbones have been found, reminding me that the Bann valley is one of the oldest inhabited areas in the country. The demesne was walled, wooded, beyond our ken; the bog was rushy and treacherous, no place for children. They said you shouldn't go near the moss-holes because 'there was no bottom in them'.

Mossbawn was bordered by the townlands of Broagh and Anahorish, townlands that are forgotten Gaelic music in the throat, *bruach* and *anach fhíor uisce*, the riverbank and the place of clear water. The names lead past the literary mists of a Celtic twilight into that civilization whose demise was effected by soldiers and administrators like Spenser and Davies, whose lifeline was bitten through when the squared-off walls of bawn and demesne dropped on the country like the jaws of a man-trap.

Yet I also looked across our fields to Grove Hill and Back Park, names that fetch the imagination in a different direction. They insist that this familiar locale is a version of pastoral and I am reminded of Davies's response to the landscape of Fermanagh—'it is so pleasant and fruitful country that if I should make a full description thereof, it would be rather taken for a poetical fiction than a true and serious narration.' Grove is a word that I associate with translations from the classics, a sunlit treeline, a tonsured hillock approached by white-robed priests. The literary word and the earthwork sentried by Scotch firs sit ill together. My illiterate ear isn't totally satisfied, as it is by another name, The Dirraghs, from *doire* as in Derry, also usually Englished as 'oak grove'. Grove and park, they do not reach me as a fibre from a tap-root but remind me of the intricate and various foliage of history and culture that I grew up beneath.

Recently at a poetry reading in Cork a student remarked, half reproachfully, that my poetry didn't sound very Celtic. The verb was probably more precise than he intended. His observation was informed by an idea of Irish poetry in English, formulated most coherently by Thomas McDonagh, a professor of English at University College, Dublin, who was shot for his part in the Easter Rising of 1916. In his view, the distinctive note of Irish poetry is struck when the rhythms and assonances of Gaelic poetry insinuate themselves into the texture of the English verse. And indeed many poets in this century, notably Austin Clarke, have applied Gaelic techniques in the making of their music and metres. I am sympathetic to the effects gained but I find the whole enterprise a bit programmatic.

Certainly the secret of being a poet, Irish or otherwise, lies in the summoning of the energies of words. But my quest for definition, while it may lead backward, is conducted in the living speech of the landscape I was born into. If you like, I began as a poet when my roots were crossed with my reading. I think of the personal and Irish pieties as vowels, and the literary awarenesses nourished on English as consonants. My hope is that the poems will be vocables adequate to my whole experience.

Guardian, 1972

II

Feeling into Words

I intend to retrace some paths into what William Wordsworth called in *The Prelude* 'the hiding places'.

> The hiding places of my power
> Seem open; I approach, and then they close;
> I see by glimpses now; when age comes on,
> May scarcely see at all, and I would give,
> While yet we may, as far as words can give,
> A substance and a life to what I feel:
> I would enshrine the spirit of the past
> For future restoration.

Implicit in those lines is a view of poetry which I think is implicit in the few poems I have written that give me any right to speak: poetry as divination, poetry as revelation of the self to the self, as restoration of the culture to itself; poems as elements of continuity, with the aura and authenticity of archaeological finds, where the buried shard has an importance that is not diminished by the importance of the buried city; poetry as a dig, a dig for finds that end up being plants.

'Digging', in fact, was the name of the first poem I wrote where I thought my feelings had got into words, or to put it more accurately, where I thought my *feel* had got into words. Its rhythms and noises still please me, although there are a couple of lines in it that have more of the theatricality of the gunslinger than the self-absorption of the digger. I wrote it in the summer of 1964, almost two years after I had begun to 'dabble in verses'. This was the first place where I felt I had done more than make an arrangement of words: I felt that I had let down a shaft into real life. The facts and surfaces of the thing were true, but more important, the excitement that came from naming them gave me a kind of insouciance and a kind of confidence. I didn't care

41

who thought what about it: somehow, it had surprised me
by coming out with a stance and an idea that I would stand
over:

> The cold smell of potato mould, the squelch and slap
> Of soggy peat, the curt cuts of an edge
> Through living roots awaken in my head.
> But I've no spade to follow men like them.

> Between my finger and my thumb
> The squat pen rests.
> I'll dig with it.

As I say, I wrote it down years ago; yet perhaps I should say
that I dug it up, because I have come to realize that it was laid
down in me years before that even. The pen/spade analogy was
the simple heart of the matter and *that* was simply a matter of
almost proverbial common sense. As a child on the road to and
from school, people used to ask you what class you were in and
how many slaps you'd got that day and invariably they ended up
with an exhortation to keep studying because 'learning's easy
carried' and 'the pen's lighter than the spade'. And the poem
does no more than allow that bud of wisdom to exfoliate,
although the significant point in this context is that at the time
of writing I was not aware of the proverbial structure at the back
of my mind. Nor was I aware that the poem was an enactment of
yet another digging metaphor that came back to me years later.
This was the rhyme we used to chant on the road to school,
though, as I have said before, we were not fully aware of what
we were dealing with:

> 'Are your praties dry
> And are they fit for digging?'
> 'Put in your spade and try,'
> Says Dirty-Faced McGuigan.

There digging becomes a sexual metaphor, an emblem of initiation, like putting your hand into the bush or robbing the nest,
one of the various natural analogies for uncovering and touching the hidden thing. I now believe that the 'Digging' poem had
for me the force of an initiation: the confidence I mentioned
arose from a sense that perhaps I could do this poetry thing too,

and having experienced the excitement and release of it once, I
was doomed to look for it again and again.

I don't want to overload 'Digging' with too much significance. It is a big coarse-grained navvy of a poem, but it is
interesting as an example—and not just as an example of what
one reviewer called 'mud-caked fingers in Russell Square', for I
don't think that the subject-matter has any particular virtue in
itself—it is interesting an example of what we call 'finding a
voice'.

Finding a voice means that you can get your own feeling into
your own words and that your words have the feel of you about
them; and I believe that it may not even be a metaphor, for a
poetic voice is probably very intimately connected with the
poet's natural voice, the voice that he hears as the ideal speaker
of the lines he is making up.

In his novel *The First Circle*, Solzhenitzyn sets the action in a
prison camp on the outskirts of Moscow where the inmates are
all highly skilled technicians forced to labour at projects
dreamed up by Stalin. The most important of these is an
attempt to devise a mechanism to bug a phone. But what is to be
special about this particular bugging device is that it will not
simply record the voice and the message but that it will identify
the essential sound patterns of the speaker's voice; it will discover, in the words of the narrative, 'what it is that makes every
human voice unique', so that no matter how the speaker disguises his accent or changes his language, the fundamental
structure of his voice will be caught. The idea was that a voice is
like a fingerprint, possessing a constant and unique signature
that can, like a fingerprint, be recorded and employed for
identification.

Now one of the purposes of a literary education as I experienced it was to turn the student's ear into a poetic bugging
device, so that a piece of verse denuded of name and date could
be identified by its diction, tropes and cadences. And this secret
policing of English verse was also based on the idea of a style as a
signature. But what I wish to suggest is that there is a connection between the core of a poet's speaking voice and the core of
his poetic voice, between his original accent and his discovered
style. I think that the discovery of a way of writing that is
natural and adequate to your sensibility depends on the

43

recovery of that essential quick which Solzhenitzyn's technicians were trying to pin down. This is the absolute register to which your proper music has to be tuned.

How, then, do you find it? In practice, you hear it coming from somebody else, you hear something in another writer's sounds that flows in through your ear and enters the echo-chamber of your head and delights your whole nervous system in such a way that your reaction will be, 'Ah, I wish I had said that, in that particular way.' This other writer, in fact, has spoken something essential to you, something you recognize instinctively as a true sounding of aspects of yourself and your experience. And your first steps as a writer will be to imitate, consciously or unconsciously, those sounds that flowed in, that in-fluence.

One of the writers who influenced me in this way was Gerard Manley Hopkins. The result of reading Hopkins at school was the desire to write, and when I first put pen to paper at university, what flowed out was what had flowed in, the bumpy alliterating music, the reporting sounds and ricochetting consonants typical of Hopkins's verse. I remember lines from a piece called 'October Thought' in which some frail bucolic images foundered under the chainmail of the pastiche:

> Starling thatch-watches, and sudden swallow
> Straight breaks to mud-nest, home-rest rafter
> Up past dry dust-drunk cobwebs, like laughter
> Ghosting the roof of bog-oak, turf-sod and rods of willow ...

and then there was 'heaven-hue, plum-blue and gorse-pricked with gold' and 'a trickling tinkle of bells well in the fold'.

Looking back on it, I believe there was a connection, not obvious at the time but, on reflection, real enough, between the heavily accented consonantal noise of Hopkins's poetic voice, and the peculiar regional characteristics of a Northern Ireland accent. The late W. R. Rodgers, another poet much lured by alliteration, said in his poem 'The Character of Ireland' that the people from his (and my) part of the world were

> an abrupt people
> who like the spiky consonants of speech
> and think the soft ones cissy; who dig
> the k and t in orchestra, detect sin

44

in sinfonia, get a kick out of
tin-cans, fricatives, fornication, staccato talk,
anything that gives or takes attack
like Micks, Teagues, tinker's gets, Vatican.

It is true that the Ulster accent is generally a staccato consonantal one. Our tongue strikes the tangent of the consonant rather
more than it rolls the circle of the vowel—Rodgers also spoke of
'the round gift of the gab in southern mouths'. It is energetic,
angular, hard-edged, and it may be because of this affinity
between my dialect and Hopkins's oddity that those first verses
turned out as they did.

I couldn't say, of course, that I had found a voice but I had
found a game. I knew the thing was only word-play, and I
hadn't even the guts to put my name to it. I called myself
Incertus, uncertain, a shy soul fretting and all that. I was in love
with words themselves, but had no sense of a poem as a whole
structure and no experience of how the successful achievement
of a poem could be a stepping stone in your life. Those verses
were what we might call 'trial-pieces', little stiff inept designs in
imitation of the master's fluent interlacing patterns, heavy-
handed clues to the whole craft.

I was getting my first sense of crafting words and for one
reason or another, words as bearers of history and mystery
began to invite me. Maybe it began very early when my mother
used to recite lists of affixes and suffixes, and Latin roots, with
their English meanings, rhymes that formed part of her school-
ing in the early part of the century. Maybe it began with the
exotic listing on the wireless dial: Stuttgart, Leipzig, Oslo,
Hilversum. Maybe it was stirred by the beautiful sprung
rhythms of the old BBC weather forecast: Dogger, Rockall,
Malin, Shetland, Faroes, Finisterre; or with the gorgeous and
inane phraseology of the catechism; or with the litany of the
Blessed Virgin that was part of the enforced poetry in our
household: Tower of Gold, Ark of the Covenant, Gate of
Heaven, Morning Star, Health of the Sick, Refuge of Sinners,
Comforter of the Afflicted. None of these things were consciously savoured at the time but I think the fact that I still recall
them with ease, and can delight in them as verbal music, means
that they were bedding the ear with a kind of linguistic hard-
core that could be built on some day.

That was the unconscious bedding, but poetry involves a
conscious savouring of words also. This came by way of reading
poetry itself, and being required to learn pieces by heart,
phrases even, like Keats's, from 'Lamia':

> and his vessel now
> Grated the quaystone with her brazen prow,

or Wordsworth's:

> All shod with steel,
> We hiss'd along the polished ice,

or Tennyson's:

> Old yew, which graspest at the stones
> That name the underlying dead,
> Thy fibres net the dreamless head,
> Thy roots are wrapped about the bones.

These were picked up in my last years at school, touchstones of
sorts, where the language could give you a kind of aural goose-
flesh. At the university I was delighted in the first weeks to meet
the moody energies of John Webster—'I'll make Italian cut-
works in their guts/If ever I return'—and later on to encounter
the pointed masonry of Anglo-Saxon verse and to learn about
the rich stratifications of the English language itself. Words
alone were certain good. I even went so far as to write these
'Lines to myself':

> In poetry I wish you would
> Avoid the lilting platitude.
> Give us poems humped and strong,
> Laced tight with thongs of song,
> Poems that explode in silence
> Without forcing, without violence.
> Whose music is strong and clear and good
> Like a saw zooming in seasoned wood.
> You should attempt concrete expression,
> Half-guessing, half-expression.

Ah well. Behind that was 'Ars Poetica', MacLeish's and Ver-
laine's, Eliot's 'objective correlative' (half understood) and
several critical essays (by myself and others) about 'concrete
realization'. At the university I kept the whole thing at arm's
length, read poetry for the noise and wrote about half a dozen
pieces for the literary magazine. But nothing happened inside

46

me. No experience. No epiphany. All craft—and not much of that—and no technique.

I think technique is different from craft. Craft is what you can learn from other verse. Craft is the skill of making. It wins competitions in the *Irish Times* or the *New Statesman*. It can be deployed without reference to the feelings or the self. It knows how to keep up a capable verbal athletic display; it can be content to be *vox et praeterea nihil*—all voice and nothing else—but not voice as in 'finding a voice'. Learning the craft is learning to turn the windlass at the well of poetry. Usually you begin by dropping the bucket halfway down the shaft and winding up a taking of air. You are miming the real thing until one day the chain draws unexpectedly tight and you have dipped into waters that will continue to entice you back. You'll have broken the skin on the pool of yourself. Your praties will be 'fit for digging'.

At that point it becomes appropriate to speak of technique rather than craft. Technique, as I would define it, involves not only a poet's way with words, his management of metre, rhythm and verbal texture; it involves also a definition of his stance towards life, a definition of his own reality. It involves the discovery of ways to go out of his normal cognitive bounds and raid the inarticulate: a dynamic alertness that mediates between the origins of feeling in memory and experience and the formal ploys that express these in a work of art. Technique entails the watermarking of your essential patterns of perception, voice and thought into the touch and texture of your lines; it is that whole creative effort of the mind's and body's resources to bring the meaning of experience within the jurisdiction of form. Technique is what turns, in Yeats's phrase, 'the bundle of accident and incoherence that sits down to breakfast' into 'an idea, something intended, complete'.

It is indeed conceivable that a poet could have a real technique and a wobbly craft—I think this was true of Alun Lewis and Patrick Kavanagh—but more often it is a case of a sure enough craft and a failure of technique. And if I were asked for a figure who represents pure technique, I would say a water diviner. You can't learn the craft of dowsing or divining—it is a gift for being in touch with what is there, hidden and real, a gift for mediating between the latent resource and the community

47

that wants it current and released. As Sir Philip Sidney notes in his *Apologie for Poetry*: 'Among the Romans a Poet was called *Vates*, which is as much as a Diviner ...'

The poem was written simply to allay an excitement and to name an experience, and at the same time to give the excitement and the experience a small *perpetuum mobile* in language itself. I quote it here, not for its own technique but for the image of technique contained in it. The diviner resembles the poet in his function of making contact with what lies hidden, and in his ability to make palpable what was sensed or raised.

The Diviner

Cut from the green hedge a forked hazel stick
That he held tight by the arms of the V:
Circling the terrain, hunting the pluck
Of water, nervous, but professionally

Unfussed. The pluck came sharp as a sting.
The rod jerked with precise convulsions,
Spring water suddenly broadcasting
Through a green hazel its secret stations.

The bystanders would ask to have a try.
He handed them the rod without a word.
It lay dead in their grasp till nonchalantly
He gripped expectant wrists. The hazel stirred.

What I had taken as matter of fact as a youngster became a matter of wonder in memory. When I look at the thing now I am pleased that it ends with a verb, 'stirred', the heart of the mystery; and I am glad that 'stirred' chimes with 'word', bringing the two functions of *vates* into the one sound.

Technique is what allows that first stirring of the mind round a word or an image or a memory to grow towards articulation: articulation not necessarily in terms of argument or explication but in terms of its own potential for harmonious self-reproduction. The seminal excitement has to be granted conditions in which, in Hopkins's words, it 'selves, goes itself ... crying/What I do is me, for that I came.' Technique ensures that the first gleam attains its proper effulgence. And I don't just mean a felicity in the choice of words to flesh the theme—that is a problem also but it is not so critical. A poem can survive stylistic blemishes but it cannot survive a still-birth. The crucial action is pre-verbal, to be able to allow the first alertness or come-hither, sensed in a blurred or incomplete way, to dilate and approach as a thought or a theme or a phrase. Robert Frost put it this way: 'a poem begins as a lump in the throat, a homesickness, a lovesickness. It finds the thought and the thought finds the words.' As far as I am concerned, technique is more vitally and sensitively connected with that first activity where the 'lump in the throat' finds 'the thought' than with 'the thought' finding 'the words'. That first emergence involves the divining, vatic, oracular function; the second, the making function. To say, as Auden did, that a poem is a 'verbal contraption' is to keep one or two tricks up your sleeve.

Traditionally an oracle speaks in riddles, yielding its truths in disguise, offering its insights cunningly. And in the practice of poetry, there is a corresponding occasion of disguise, a protean, chameleon moment when the lump in the throat takes protective colouring in the new element of thought. One of the best documented occasions in the canon of English poetry, as far as this process is concerned, is a poem that survived in spite of its blemish. In fact, the blemish has earned it a peculiar fame:

> High on a mountain's highest ridge,
> Where oft the stormy winter gale
> Cuts like a scythe, while through the clouds
> It sweeps from vale to vale;
> Not five yards from the mountain path,
> This thorn you on your left espy;
> And to the left, three yards beyond,
> You see a little muddy pond
> Of water never dry;
> I've measured it from side to side:
> 'Tis three feet long and two feet wide.

Those two final lines were probably more ridiculed than any other lines in *The Lyrical Ballads* yet Wordsworth maintained 'they ought to be liked'. That was in 1815, seventeen years after the poem had been composed; but five years later he changed them to 'Though but of compass small, and bare/To thirsting suns and parching air'. Craft, in more senses than one.

Yet far more important than the revision, for the purposes of this discussion, is Wordsworth's account of the poem's genesis. 'The Thorn', he told Isabella Fenwick in 1843,

> arose out of my observing on the ridge of Quantock Hills, on a stormy day, a thorn which I had often passed in calm and bright weather without noticing it. I said to myself, 'Cannot I by some invention do as much to make this thorn permanently an impressive object, as the storm has made it to my eyes at this moment?' I began the poem accordingly, and composed it with great rapidity.

The storm, in other words, was nature's technique for granting the thorn-tree its epiphany, awakening in Wordsworth that engendering, heightened state which he describes at the beginning of *The Prelude*—again in relation to the inspiring influence of wind:

> For I, methought, while the sweet breath of Heaven
> Was blowing on my body, felt within
> A corresponding, mild, creative breeze,
> A vital breeze which travell'd gently on
> O'er things which it had made, and is become
> A tempest, a redundant energy
> Vexing its own creation.

This is exactly the kind of mood in which he would have 'composed with great rapidity'; the measured recollection of the letter where he makes the poem sound as if it were written to the thesis propounded (retrospectively) in the Preface of 1800— 'cannot I by some invention make this thorn permanently an impressive object?'—probably tones down an instinctive, instantaneous recognition into a rational procedure. The technical triumph was to discover a means of allowing his slightly abnormal, slightly numinous vision of the thorn to 'deal out its being'.

What he did to turn 'the bundle of accident and incoherence' of that moment into 'something intended, complete' was to find, in Yeats's language, a mask. The poem as we have it is a ballad in which the speaker is a garrulous superstitious man, a sea captain, according to Wordsworth, who connects the thorn with murder and distress. For Wordsworth's own apprehension of the tree, he instinctively recognized, was basically superstitious: it was a standing over, a survival in his own sensibility of a

magical way of responding to the natural world, of reading
phenomena as signs, occurrences requiring divination. And in
order to dramatize this, to transpose the awakened appetites in
his consciousness into the satisfactions of a finished thing, he
needed his 'objective correlative'. To make the thorn 'permanently an impressive object', images and ideas from different
parts of his conscious and unconscious mind were attracted by
almost magnetic power. The thorn in its new, wind-tossed
aspect had become a field of force.

Into this field were drawn memories of what the ballads call
'the cruel mother' who murders her own baby:

> She leaned her back against a thorn
> All around the loney-o
> And there her little babe was born
> Down by the greenwood side-o

is how a surviving version runs in Ireland. But there have
always been variations on this pattern of the woman who kills
her baby and buries it. And the ballads are also full of briars and
roses and thorns growing out of graves in symbolic token of the
life and death of the buried one. So in Wordsworth's imagination the thorn grew into a symbol of tragic, feverish death, and
to voice this the ballad mode came naturally; he donned the
traditional mask of the tale-teller, legitimately credulous, entering and enacting a convention. The poem itself is a rapid and
strange foray where Wordsworth discovered a way of turning
the 'lump in the throat' into a 'thought', discovered a set of
images, cadences and sounds that amplified his original
visionary excitement into 'a redundant energy/Vexing its own
creation':

> And some had sworn an oath that she
> Should be to public justice brought;
> And for the little infant's bones
> With spades they would have sought.
> But then the beauteous hill of moss
> Before their eyes began to stir;
> And for full fifty yards around
> The grass it shook upon the ground.

'The Thorn' is a nicely documented example of feeling getting
into words, in ways that paralleled much in my own experience;

although I must say that it is hard to discriminate between feeling getting into words and words turning into feeling, and it is only on posthumous occasions like this that the distinction arises. Moreover, it is dangerous for a writer to become too self-conscious about his own processes: to name them too definitively may have the effect of confining them to what is named. A poem always has elements of accident about it, which can be made the subject of inquest afterwards, but there is always a risk in conducting your own inquest: you might begin to believe the coroner in yourself rather than put your trust in the man in you who is capable of the accident. Robert Graves's 'Dance of Words' puts this delightfully:

> To make them move, you should start from lightning
> And not forecast the rhythm: rely on chance
> Or so-called chance for its bright emergence
> Once lightning interpenetrates the dance.
>
> Grant them their own traditional steps and postures
> But see they dance it out again and again
> Until only lightning is left to puzzle over—
> The choreography plain and the theme plain.

What we are engaged upon here is a way of seeing that turns the lightning into 'the visible discharge of electricity between cloud and cloud or between cloud and ground' rather than its own puzzling, brilliant self. There is nearly always an element of the bolt from the blue about a poem's origin.

When I called my second book *Door into the Dark* I intended to gesture towards this idea of poetry as a point of entry into the buried life of the feelings or as a point of exit for it. Words themselves are doors; Janus is to a certain extent their deity, looking back to a ramification of roots and associations and forward to a clarification of sense and meaning. And just as Wordsworth sensed a secret asking for release in the thorn, so in *Door into the Dark* there are a number of poems that arise out of the almost unnameable energies that, for me, hovered over certain bits of language and landscape.

The poem 'Undine', for example. It was the dark pool of the sound of the word that first took me: if our auditory imaginations were sufficiently attuned to plumb and sound a vowel, to unite the most primitive and civilized associations, the word 'undine' would probably suffice as a poem in itself. *Unda*, a wave, *undine*, a water-woman—a litany of undines would have ebb and flow, water and woman, wave and tide, fulfilment and exhaustion in its very rhythms. But, old two-faced vocable that it is, I discovered a more precise definition once, by accident, in a dictionary. An undine is a water-sprite who has to marry a human being and have a child by him before she can become human. With that definition, the lump in the throat, or rather the thump in the ear, *undine*, became a thought, a field of force that called up other images. One of these was an orphaned memory, without a context, obviously a very early one, of watching a man clearing out an old spongy growth from a drain between two fields, focusing in particular on the way the water, in the cleared-out place, as soon as the shovelfuls of sludge had been removed, the way the water began to run free, rinse itself clean of the soluble mud and make its own little channels and currents. And this image was gathered into a more conscious reading of the myth as being about the liberating, humanizing effect of sexual encounter. Undine was a cold girl who got what the dictionary called a soul through the experience of physical love. So the poem uttered itself out of that nexus—more short-winded than 'The Thorn', with less red*undant* energy, but still escaping, I hope, from my incoherence into the voice of the undine herself:

> He slashed the briars, shovelled up grey silt
> To give me right of way in my own drains
> And I ran quick for him, cleaned out my rust.
>
> He halted, saw me finally disrobed,
> Running clear, with apparent unconcern.
> Then he walked by me. I rippled and I churned
>
> Where ditches intersected near the river
> Until he dug a spade deep in my flank
> And took me to him. I swallowed his trench
>
> Gratefully, dispersing myself for love
> Down in his roots, climbing his brassy grain—
> But once he knew my welcome, I alone

Could give him subtle increase and reflection.
He explored me so completely, each limb
Lost its cold freedom. Human, warmed to him.

I once said it was a myth about agriculture, about the way water is tamed and humanized when streams become irrigation canals, when water becomes involved with seed. And maybe that is as good an explanation as any. The paraphrasable extensions of a poem can be as protean as possible as long as its elements remain firm. Words can allow you that two-faced approach also. They stand smiling at the audience's way of reading them and winking back at the poet's way of using them.

Behind this, of course, there is a good bit of symbolist theory. Yet in practice, you proceed by your own experience of what it is to write what you consider a successful poem. You survive in your own esteem not by the corroboration of theory but by the trust in certain moments of satisfaction which you know intuitively to be moments of extension. You are confirmed by the visitation of the last poem and threatened by the elusiveness of the next one, and the best moments are those when your mind seems to implode and words and images rush of their own accord into the vortex. Which happened to me once when the line 'We have no prairies' drifted into my head at bedtime, and loosened a fall of images that constitute the poem 'Bogland', the last one in *Door into the Dark*.

I had been vaguely wishing to write a poem about bogland, chiefly because it is a landscape that has a strange assuaging effect on me, one with associations reaching back into early childhood. We used to hear about bog-butter, butter kept fresh for a great number of years under the peat. Then when I was at school the skeleton of an elk had been taken out of a bog nearby and a few of our neighbours had got their photographs in the paper, peering out across its antlers. So I began to get an idea of bog as the memory of the landscape, or as a landscape that remembered everything that happened in and to it. In fact, if you go round the National Museum in Dublin, you will realize that a great proportion of the most cherished material heritage of Ireland was 'found in a bog'. Moreover, since memory was the faculty that supplied me with the first quickening of my own poetry, I had a tentative unrealized need to make a congruence between memory and bogland and, for the want of a better

word, our national consciousness. And it all released itself after
'We have no prairies . . .'—but we have bogs.

At that time I was teaching modern literature in Queen's
University, Belfast, and had been reading about the frontier
and the west as an important myth in the American consciousness, so I set up—or rather, laid down—the bog as an answer-
ing Irish myth. I wrote it quickly the next morning, having
slept on my excitement, and revised it on the hoof, from line to
line, as it came:

> We have no prairies
> To slice a big sun at evening—
> Everywhere the eye concedes to
> Encroaching horizon,
>
> Is wooed into the cyclops' eye
> Of a tarn. Our unfenced country
> Is bog that keeps crusting
> Between the sights of the sun.
>
> They've taken the skeleton
> Of the great Irish Elk
> Out of the peat, set it up
> An astounding crate full of air.
>
> Butter sunk under
> More than a hundred years
> Was recovered salty and white.
> The ground itself is kind, black butter
>
> Melting and opening underfoot,
> Missing its last definition
> By millions of years.
> They'll never dig coal here,
>
> Only the waterlogged trunks
> Of great firs, soft as pulp.
> Our pioneers keep striking
> Inwards and downwards,
>
> Every layer they strip
> Seems camped on before.
> The bogholes might be Atlantic seepage.
> The wet centre is bottomless.

Again, as in the case of 'Digging', the seminal impulse had been unconscious. What generated the poem about memory was something lying beneath the very floor of memory, something I only connected with the poem months after it was written, which was a warning that older people would give us about going into the bog. They were afraid we might fall into the pools in the old workings so they put it about (and we believed them) that *there was no bottom* in the bog-holes. Little did they—or I—know that I would filch it for the last line of a book.

There was also in that book a poem called 'Requiem for the Croppies' which was written in 1966 when most poets in Ireland were straining to celebrate the anniversary of the 1916 Rising. That rising was the harvest of seeds sown in 1798, when revolutionary republican ideals and national feeling coalesced in the doctrines of Irish republicanism and in the rebellion of 1798 itself—unsuccessful and savagely put down. The poem was born of and ended with an image of resurrection based on the fact that some time after the rebels were buried in common graves, these graves began to sprout with young barley, growing up from barley corn which the 'croppies' had carried in their pockets to eat while on the march. The oblique implication was that the seeds of violent resistance sowed in the Year of Liberty had flowered in what Yeats called 'the right rose tree' of 1916. I did not realize at the time that the original heraldic murderous encounter between Protestant yeoman and Catholic rebel was to be initiated again in the summer of 1969, in Belfast, two months after the book was published.

From that moment the problems of poetry moved from being simply a matter of achieving the satisfactory verbal icon to being a search for images and symbols adequate to our predicament. I do not mean liberal lamentation that citizens should feel compelled to murder one another or deploy their different military arms over the matter of nomenclatures such as British or Irish. I do not mean public celebrations or execrations of resistance or atrocity—although there is nothing necessarily unpoetic about such celebration, if one thinks of Yeats's 'Easter 1916'. I mean that I felt it imperative to discover a field of force in which, without abandoning fidelity to the processes and experience of poetry as I have outlined them, it would be possible to encompass the perspectives of a humane reason and at the same time to grant the religious intensity of the violence its deplorable authenticity and complexity. And when I say religious, I am not thinking simply of the sectarian division. To some extent the enmity can be viewed as a struggle between the cults and devotees of a god and a goddess. There is an indigenous territorial numen, a tutelar of the whole island, call her Mother Ireland, Kathleen Ni Houlihan, the poor old woman, the Shan Van Vocht, whatever; and her sovereignty has been temporarily usurped or infringed by a new male cult whose founding fathers were Cromwell, William of Orange and Edward Carson, and whose godhead is incarnate in a rex or caesar resident in a palace in London. What we have is the tail-end of a struggle in a province between territorial piety and imperial power.

Now I realize that this idiom is remote from the agnostic world of economic interest whose iron hand operates in the velvet glove of 'talks between elected representatives', and remote from the political manoeuvres of power-sharing; but it is not remote from the psychology of the Irishmen and Ulstermen who do the killing, and not remote from the bankrupt psychology and mythologies implicit in the terms Irish Catholic and Ulster Protestant. The question, as ever, is 'How with this rage shall beauty hold a plea?' And my answer is, by offering 'befitting emblems of adversity'.

Some of these emblems I found in a book that was published in English translation, appositely, the year the killing started, in 1969. And again appositely, it was entitled *The Bog People*. It was chiefly concerned with preserved bodies of men and women found in the bogs of Jutland, naked, strangled or with their throats cut, disposed under the peat since early Iron Age times. The author, P. V. Glob, argues convincingly that a number of these, and in particular the Tollund Man, whose head is now preserved near Aarhus in the museum at Silkeburg, were ritual sacrifices to the Mother Goddess, the goddess of the ground who needed new bridegrooms each winter to bed with her in her sacred place, in the bog, to ensure the renewal and fertility of the territory in the spring. Taken in relation to the tradition of Irish political martyrdom for that cause whose icon is Kathleen Ni Houlihan, this is more than an archaic barbarous rite: it is an archetypal pattern. And the unforgettable photographs of these victims blended in my mind with photographs of atrocities, past and present, in the long rites of Irish political and religious struggles. When I wrote this poem, I had a completely new sensation, one of fear. It was a vow to go on pilgrimage and I felt as it came to me—and again it came quickly—that unless I was deeply in earnest about what I was saying, I was simply invoking dangers for myself. It is called 'The Tollund Man':

I

Some day I will go to Aarhus
To see his peat-brown head,
The mild pods of his eye-lids,
His pointed skin cap.

In the flat country nearby
Where they dug him out,
His last gruel of winter seeds
Caked in his stomach,

Naked except for
The cap, noose and girdle,
I will stand a long time.
Bridegroom to the goddess,

She tightened her torc on him
And opened her fen,
Those dark juices working
Him to a saint's kept body,

Trove of the turfcutters'
Honeycombed workings.
Now his stained face
Reposes at Aarhus.

II

I could risk blasphemy,
Consecrate the cauldron bog
Our holy ground and pray
Him to make germinate

The scattered, ambushed
Flesh of labourers,
Stockinged corpses
Laid out in the farmyards,

58

Tell-tale skin and teeth
Flecking the sleepers
Of four young brothers, trailed
For miles along the lines.

III

Something of his sad freedom
As he rode the tumbril
Should come to me, driving,
Saying the names

Tollund, Grauballe, Nebelgard,
Watching the pointing hands
Of country people,
Not knowing their tongue.

Out there in Jutland
In the old man-killing parishes
I will feel lost,
Unhappy and at home.

And just how persistent the barbaric attitudes are, not only in
the slaughter but in the psyche, I discovered, again when the
frisson of the poem itself had passed, and indeed after I had
fulfilled the vow and gone to Jutland, 'the holy blisful martyr
for to seke'. I read the following in a chapter on 'The Religion of
the Pagan Celts' by the Celtic scholar, Anne Ross:

> Moving from sanctuaries and shrines . . . we come now to consider
> the nature of the actual deities. . . . But before going on to look at
> the nature of some of the individual deities and their cults, one can
> perhaps bridge the gap as it were by considering a symbol which, in
> its way, sums up the whole of Celtic pagan religion and is as
> representative of it as is, for example, the sign of the cross in
> Christian contexts. This is the symbol of the severed human head;
> in all its various modes of iconographic representation and verbal
> presentation, one may find the hard core of Celtic religion. It is
> indeed . . . a kind of shorthand symbol for the entire religious
> outlook of the pagan Celts.*

My sense of occasion and almost awe as I vowed to go to pray to
the Tollund Man and assist at his enshrined head had a longer
ancestry than I had at the time realized.

* *Pagan Celtic Britain: Studies in Iconography and Tradition*, Routledge, 1967.

I began by suggesting that my point of view involved poetry as divination, as a restoration of the culture to itself. In Ireland in this century it has involved for Yeats and many others an attempt to define and interpret the present by bringing it into significant relationship with the past, and I believe that effort in our present circumstances has to be urgently renewed. But here we stray from the realm of technique into the realm of tradition; to forge a poem is one thing, to forge the uncreated conscience of the race, as Stephen Dedalus put it, is quite another and places daunting pressures and responsibilities on anyone who would risk the name of poet.

Lecture given at the Royal Society of Literature,
October 1974

The Makings of a Music

Reflections on Wordsworth and Yeats

What interests me is the relationship between the almost physiological operations of a poet composing and the music of the finished poem. I want to explore the way that certain postures and motions within the poet's incubating mind affect the posture of the voice and the motion of rhythms in the language of the poem itself. I want to see how far we can go in seeking the origins of a poet's characteristic 'music'.

I chose the word 'makings' for the title because it gestures towards the testings and hesitations of the workshop, the approaches towards utterance, the discovery of lines and then the intuitive extension of the vital element in those lines over a whole passage. If you like, I am interested in the way Valéry's two kinds of poetic lines, *les vers donnés* and *les vers calculés*, are combined. The given line, the phrase or cadence which haunts the ear and the eager parts of the mind, this is the tuning fork to which the whole music of the poem is orchestrated, that out of which the overall melodies are worked for or calculated. It is my impression that this haunting or *donné* occurs to all poets in much the same way, arbitrarily, with a sense of promise, as an alertness, a hankering, a readiness. It is also my impression that the quality of the music in the finished poem has to do with the way the poet proceeds to respond to his *donné*. If he surrenders to it, allows himself to be carried by its initial rhythmic suggestiveness, to become somnambulist after its invitations, then we will have a music not unlike Wordsworth's, hypnotic, swimming with the current of its form rather than against it. If, on the other hand, instead of surrendering to the drift of the original generating rhythm, the poet seeks to discipline it, to

61

harness its energies in order to drive other parts of his mind into motion, then we will have a music not unlike Yeats's, affirmative, seeking to master rather than to mesmerize the ear, swimming strongly against the current of its form.

Of course, in any poetic music, there will always be two contributory elements. There is that part of the poetry which takes its structure and beat, its play of metre and rhythms, its diction and allusiveness, from the literary tradition. The poetry that Wordsworth and Yeats had read as adolescents and as young men obviously laid down certain structures in their ear, structures that gave them certain kinds of aural expectations for their own writings. And we are all used to the study of this kind of influence: indeed, as T. S. Eliot has attested, we have not developed our taste in poetry until we can recognize with pleasure the way an individual talent has foraged in the tradition. But there is a second element in a poet's music, derived not from the literate parts of his mind but from its illiterate parts, dependent not upon what Jacques Maritain called his 'intellectual baggage' but upon what I might call his instinctual ballast. What kinds of noise assuage him, what kinds of music pleasure or repel him, what messages the receiving stations of his senses are happy to pick up from the world around him and what ones they automatically block out—all this unconscious activity, at the pre-verbal level, is entirely relevant to the intonations and appeasements offered by a poet's music.

We have developed methods for tracing and expressing the relevance and significance of the first kind of influence, the literary influence, and much of the illuminating work on Wordsworth has been in this area. I remember with particular gratitude the late W. J. Harvey's inaugural lecture at Queen's University, in which he analysed the opening lines of *The Prelude* to show how those lines were influenced by the closing lines of *Paradise Lost*. Once it has been pointed out to us that Wordsworth's joy in open country and his sense of release from the bondage of the city are consciously set in the penumbra of Adam and Eve's expulsion from Eden, and that the language of Wordsworth's lines invites us to read his freedom in the context of that expulsion, then the whole lift of the passage is increased, and the wave of Wordsworth's feeling is rendered seismic by one discreet literary allusion.

But I seek my text a little further on in that passage, where the poet tells us that his poetry came to him on this occasion spontaneously and that he poured it out, told it to the open fields. Then come these four lines, precise, honest, revealing:

> My own voice cheered me, and, far more, the mind's
> Internal echo of the imperfect sound;
> To both I listened, drawing from them both
> A cheerful confidence in things to come.

Although Wordsworth is here describing the activity of composing aloud, of walking and talking, what the poetry reaches into is the activity of listening. 'My own voice cheered me'—in the words of the old joke, he is entranced by the exuberance of his own verbosity. The act of composition is a cheering one. But even though he is listening to the sound of his own voice, he realizes that this spoken music is just a shadow of the unheard melody, 'the mind's internal echo'. He is drawn into himself even as he speaks himself out, and it is this mesmerized attention to the echoes and invitations within that constitutes his poetic confidence. We need only recall for contrast the way W. H. Auden addressed himself to the discussion of the act of writing, always tackling it in terms of metre, stanza forms, philology, always keeping in front of us the idea of the poem as 'a verbal contraption', to see how intimately and exactly Wordsworth is touching into the makings of his music in those lines.

What we are presented with is a version of composition as listening, as a wise passiveness, a surrender to energies that spring within the centre of the mind, not composition as an active pursuit by the mind's circumference of something already at the centre. The more attentively Wordsworth listens in, the more cheerfully and abundantly he speaks out.

We have ample evidence of Wordsworth's practice of composing aloud. In *The Prelude* he tells us how he paced the woods with his dog running a bit ahead of him, so that the dog's barking would warn him of strangers and he could then quieten his iambic drone and not be taken for an idiot. We have also the evidence gathered by the Reverend Canon Rawnsley among the peasantry of Westmorland that he was not always successful in passing undetected:

63

But thear was anudder thing as kep' fwoaks off, he hed a terr'ble girt deep voice . . . I've knoan folks, village lads and lasses, coming ower by t'auld road aboon what runs fra Grasmer to Rydal, flayt a'most to death there by t' Wishing Gate to hear t' girt voice a groanin' and mutterin' and thunderin' of a still evening. And he had a way of standin' quite still by t' rock there in t' path under Rydal, and fwoaks could hear sounds like a wild beast coming frat' rocks, and childer were scared fit to be dead a'most.

And elsewhere Rawnsley's informant told of Mrs. Wordsworth's difficulties also:

Mrs. Wudsworth would say, 'Ring the bell,' but he wouldn't stir, bless ye. 'Goa and see what he's doing,' she'd say, and we wad goa up to study door and hear him a mumbling and bumming through hit. 'Dinner's ready, sir,' I'd ca' out, but he'd goa mumbling on like a deaf man, ya see. And sometimes Mrs. Wordsworth 'ud say, 'Goa and brek a bottle, or let a dish fall just outside door in passage.' Eh dear, that maistly wad bring him out, wad that.

But the most instructive account of the poet's habits is surely the one given by Hazlitt, who visited the Wordsworths at Alfoxden in June 1798. Hazlitt heard the poetry read first by Coleridge and then by Wordsworth. Admittedly, he does not actually witness Wordsworth in the process of composition, but he does tell us about the quality and sway of the poet's speaking voice in his essay 'My First Acquaintance with the Poets':

We went over to Alfoxden again the day following, and Wordsworth read us the story of *Peter Bell* in the open air; and the comment made upon it by his face and voice was very different from that of some later critics! Whatever might be thought of the poem, 'his face was a book where men might read strange matters,' and he announced the fate of his hero in prophetic tones. There is a *chaunt* in the recitation of both Coleridge and Wordsworth, which acts as a spell upon the hearer, and disarms the judgement. Perhaps they have deceived themselves by making habitual use of this ambiguous accompaniment. Coleridge's manner is more full, animated and varied; Wordsworth's more equable, sustained and internal. The one might be termed more *dramatic*, the other more *lyrical*. Coleridge has told me that he himself liked to compose in walking over uneven ground, or breaking through the straggling branches of a copse wood; whereas Wordsworth always wrote (if he could) walking up and down a straight gravel walk, or in some spot where the continuity of his verse met with no collateral interruption.

Wordsworth's chaunt acted as a spell upon the hearer, whether that hearer were Hazlitt or Wordsworth himself. It *en*chaunted. It was 'equable, sustained, internal', three adjectives which we might apply to the motion of Wordsworth's blank verse also. The continuity of the thing was what was important, the onward inward pouring out, up and down the gravel path, the crunch and scuffle of the gravel working like a metre or a metronome under the rhythms of the ongoing chaunt, those 'trances of thought and mountings of the mind' somehow aided by the automatic, monotonous turns and returns of the walk, the length of the path acting like the length of the line. And I imagine that the swing of the poet's body contributed as well to the sway of the voice, for Hazlitt tells us that 'there was something of a roll, a lounge in his gait, not unlike his own Peter Bell.' The poet as ploughman, if you like, and the suggestive etymology of the word 'verse' itself is pertinent in this context. 'Verse' comes from the Latin *versus* which could mean a line of poetry but could also mean the turn that a ploughman made at the head of the field as he finished one furrow and faced back into another. Wordsworth on the gravel path, to-ing and fro-ing like a ploughman up and down a field, his voice rising and falling between the measure of his pentameters, unites the old walking meaning of *versus* with the newer, talking sense of verse. Furthermore, Wordsworth's *poetic* voice, the first voice of his poetry, that voice in which we overhear him talking to himself, the motions of this voice remind me powerfully of the motions of plough-horses as described by the poet Edwin Muir:

> Their hooves like pistons in an ancient mill
> Move up and down, yet seem as standing still.

The high moments of Wordsworth's poetry occur when the verse has carried us forward and onward to a point where line by line we do not proceed but hang in a kind of suspended motion, sustained by the beat of the verse as a hanging bird is sustained by the beat of its wing, but, like the bird, holding actively to one point of vantage, experiencing a prolonged moment of equilibrium during which we feel ourselves to be conductors of the palpable energies of earth and sky:

> Oh, when I have hung
> Above the raven's nest, by knots of grass

65

Or half-inch fissures in the slippery rock
But ill sustained, and almost, as it seemed
Suspended by the blast which blew amain,
Shouldering the naked crag, oh, at that time,
While on the perilous ridge I hung alone,
With what strange utterance did the loud dry wind
Blow through my ears; the sky seemed not a sky
Of earth, and with what motion moved the clouds.

This is perhaps an obvious moment, when the wind of heaven
and the 'corresponding mild creative breeze' of inspiration sustain the voice and suspend the consciousness in its hovering.
But it does not always require such extreme sensation to generate the trance. For example, at the end of that 'equable, sustained internal' narrative 'The Ruined Cottage', what Wordsworth calls 'the calm oblivious tendencies/Of nature' pervade
the music, a music of coming to rest, of understanding:

She sleeps in the calm earth, and peace is here.
I well remember that those very plumes,
Those weeds, and the high spear grass on that wall,
By mist and silent raindrops silvered o'er,
As once I passed, did to my mind convey
So still an image of tranquillity,
So calm and still, and looked so beautiful
Amid the uneasy thoughts which filled my mind,
That what we feel of sorrow and despair
From ruin and from change, and all the grief
The passing shows of being leave behind,
Appeared an idle dream that could not live
Where meditation was. I turned away
And walked along my road in happiness.

We know that the phrase 'the still, sad music of humanity' will
apply to this, but it is too abstract, not kinetic enough. There is
a cumulative movement in the Pedlar's lines that does not so
much move the narrative forward as intensify the lingering
meditation, just as the up and down walking does not forward a
journey but habituates the body to a kind of dreamy rhythm.
And in this entranced state, the casual concerns of the mind, the
proper sorrow for the wounded life of Margaret imaged in the
overgrown cottage garden, such things are allayed by apprehensions of a longer, deeper tranquillity. To put it another way,
'the one life of Joy' imbues the music, is intoned by it, and can

be apprehended from it. And nowhere do we experience this more potently than in the eight lines of 'A slumber did my spirit seal':

> A slumber did my spirit seal;
>   I had no human fears:
> She seemed a thing that could not feel
>   The touch of earthly years.
>
> No motion has she now, no force;
>   She neither hears nor sees;
> Rolled round in earth's diurnal course
>   With rocks, and stones, and trees.

The music begins with 'slumber' and ends with 'diurnal', and the eight lines turn on the poles of those sturdy vowels as surely, slowly, totally as the earth turning. Unless we can hear the power and dream in the line 'Rolled round in earth's diurnal course', I do not think we can ever properly hear Wordsworth's music. The quintessential sound of it is in 'diurnal', a word that comes up again at the end of the skating passage in *The Prelude*:

> Not seldom from the uproar I retired
> Into a silent bay, or sportively
> Glanced sideway, leaving the tumultuous throng,
> To cut across the reflex of a star
> That fled, and, flying still before me, gleamed
> Upon the glassy plain; and oftentimes,
> When we had given our bodies to the wind,
> And all the shadowy banks on either side
> Came sweeping through the darkness, spinning still
> The rapid line of motion, then at once
> Have I, reclining back upon my heels,
> Stopped short; yet still the solitary cliffs
> Wheeled by me—even as if the earth had rolled
> With visible motion her diurnal round!
> Behind me did they stretch in solemn train,
> Feebler and feebler, and I stood and watched
> Till all was tranquil as a dreamless sleep.

The exhilaration of the skating, the vitality of the verbs, 'gleaming', 'sweeping', 'spinning', 'wheeling', the narrative push, the *cheerfulness*, to use one of the poet's favourite positive words—all these things have their part to play in the overall effect of this writing. But what distinguishes it as Words-worthian is the gradual allaying of the sensation which is not, however, a diminution of awareness. It is as if a lens of apprehension opens wide and holds open. It is achieved by pacing, a slow, gathering but not climactic movement, repetit-ive but not monotonous, a walking movement. We might say, in fact, that Wordsworth at his best, no less than at his worst, is a pedestrian poet. As his poetic feet repeat his footfalls, the earth seems to be a treadmill that he turns; the big diurnal roll is sensed through the poetic beat and the world moves like a waterwheel under the fall of his voice.

I introduce the water metaphor because any account of Wordsworth's music must sooner or later come to the river, but before we do so, I want to linger in the wood above Dove Cottage where the poet occasionally composed. At the moment all is quiet there, but it is an active quiet, the late morning of 29 April 1802:

> We then went to John's Grove, sate a while at first. Afterwards William lay, and I lay in the trench under the fence—he with his eyes shut and listening to the waterfalls and the birds. There was no one waterfall above another—it was a sound of waters in the air—the voice of the air. William heard me breathing and rustling now and then but we both lay still and unseen by one another. He thought it would be as sweet thus to lie in the grave, and hear the *peaceful* sounds of the earth and just to know that our dear friends were near.

Dorothy and her brother are as intimate with process here as the babes in the wood, and if there is something erotic about the rustling of those leaves, there is something cthonic about the energies fundamental to the whole experience. Phrases like 'diurnal course' and 'diurnal roll' are underwritten by sensation and take their lifeline from moments like this. The couple listen, they surrender, the noise of water and the voice of the air minister to them. The quick of this moment is like the quick of the poem 'A slumber did my spirit seal': it dramatizes the idea of 'wise passiveness' and makes the listening ear as capable of gathering might into itself as Yeats's 'gazing heart'. All the typical Wordsworthian verbs have been guaranteed: powers sink in, mould, impress, frame, minister, enter unawares.

Wordsworth had to grope along the grains of the language to

find the makings of a music that would render not so much what Hopkins called the inscape as the instress of things, known physically and intuitively at such times. His great strength and originality as a writer came first of all from his trusting the validity of his experience, from his courageous and visionary determination to *ériger en lois ses impressions personnels*. But the paraphrasable content of Wordsworth's philosophy of nature would remain inert had he not discovered the sounds proper to his sense. Nature forms the heart that watches and receives but until the voice of the poet has been correspondingly attuned, we cannot believe what we hear. And so we come to the beautiful conception of the River Derwent as tutor of his poetic ear. The tongue of the river, he implies, licked him into poetic shape; the essential capacity was, from the beginning, the capacity to listen:

> Was it for this
> That one, the fairest of all rivers, loved
> To blend his murmurs with my nurse's song,
> And from his alder shades and rocky falls,
> And from his fords and shallows, sent a voice
> That flowed along my dreams? For this didst thou,
> O Derwent, travelling over the green plains
> Near my 'sweet birth place', didst thou, beauteous stream,
> Make ceaseless music through the night and day
> Which with its steady cadence tempering
> Our human waywardness, composed my thoughts
> To more than infant softness, giving me
> Among the fretful dwellings of mankind
> A knowledge, a dim earnest, of the calm
> Which Nature breathes among the fields and groves?
> Beloved Derwent, fairest of all streams,
> Was it for this that I, a four years child,
> A naked boy, among thy silent pools
> Made one long bathing of a summer's day,
> Basked in the sun, or plunged into thy streams,
> Alternate, all a summer's day, or coursed
> Over the sandy fields, and dashed with flowers
> Of yellow grunsel; or, when crag and hill,
> The woods, and distant Skiddaw's lofty height,
> Were bronzed with a deep radiance, stood alone
> A naked savage in the thunder shower?

As in the other passages already quoted, the movement of this one also enacts the insights it presents. The river flows into dreams and composes. The passage flows, shifts through times and scenes, mixes, drifts and comes to rest with the child composed into a stilled consciousness, a living tuning fork planted between wood and hill, bronzed in the sunset.

Moreover, in that original cluster of sound and image which Wordsworth divines at the roots of his poetic voice—a river streaming hypnotically in the background, a stilled listener hovering between waking and dreaming—in this cluster of sound and image we find prefigured other moments which were definitive in his life as a poet and which found definition in his distinctive music. I am thinking of the soldier whom he encounters at dawn in Book IV of *The Prelude*, and of the Leech Gatherer; and, in particular, of the way his listening to their speech becomes a listening in and sounding forth of a something else, that something which deeply interfuses silence with sound, stillness with movement, talk with trance, and which is radical to the sound and sense he makes as a poet:

> The old Man still stood talking by my side;
> But now his voice to me was like a stream
> Scarce heard; nor word from word could I divide;
> And the whole body of the Man did seem
> Like one whom I had met with in a dream;
> Or like a man from some far region sent,
> To give me human strength, by apt admonishment.

I hope I am not indulging in special pleading when I draw attention to the rhyming of 'stream' and 'dream', and notice that shortly after this 'feet' is rhymed with 'repeat', and then 'me', 'silently' and 'continually' are harmonized. I am convinced that these words are conducting us towards something essential to the poetry.

I have been talking about the 'first voice' of Wordsworth's poetry, as that term was defined by Gottfried Benn and approved by T. S. Eliot, that is 'the voice of the poet talking to himself—or to nobody', the voice that is found to express 'a dark embryo', 'a something germinating in him for which he must find words.' Admittedly there is another voice in Wordsworth, which he was conscious of himself and which comes about, when, as he says in his Preface to *Lyrical Ballads*, the poet

> bring[s] his feelings near to those of the persons whose feelings he describes, nay, for short periods of time perhaps . . . let[s] himself slip into an entire delusion, and even confound[s] and identifies his feelings with theirs.

'Peter Bell', 'The Idiot Boy' and 'The Thorn' come to mind, yet in these poems I suspect that there was nothing fundamentally dramatic about Wordsworth's surrender to the speech of the character. It was not a question of the poet's voice performing a part but of the poet's voice being possessed; it was not a question of technical cool, of finding a dramatic pitch, rather a matter of sympathetic warmth, of sinking into a mood of evocation. And in this the Wordsworthian process differs radically from the Yeatsian, just as the satisfaction and scope of their musics differ.

Both Yeats and Wordsworth liked to speak their lines, both intoned, yet both had difficulty in the actual writing of the poem. I have stressed the primary generating surrender that Wordsworth seems to have made to his *donnés* because it seems to me that that was definitive of his music. Yet it is also true that Dorothy's *Journals* are full of evidence that the composition of long poems like 'Michael' affected him nervously and physically; he became sick and exhausted by the strain of the writing, and Mary Moorman even speculates that he may have felt his career as a poet menaced by these symptoms. Nevertheless, the strain does not show in the verse and Wordsworth continued to think of the poetic act as essentially an act of complaisance with natural impulses and tendencies.

It is otherwise with Yeats. With him, the act is not one of complaisance but of control. In fact, one of the earliest references to Yeats's habit of composing aloud is in a letter written by his father in 1884, and there the father speaks of his son's procedure as 'manipulation'. 'His bad metres arise', J. B. Yeats wrote, 'from his composing in a loud voice manipulating of course the quantities to his taste.' Where we can think of Wordsworth going into a trance, mesmerized by the sound of his own voice, we have to think of Yeats testing and trying out different voices and deciding on which will come most resonantly from

71

the mask. Consider, for example, his performance in the following passage, written near the end of his career:

> Every now and then, when something has stirred my imagination, I begin talking to myself. I speak in my own person and dramatize myself, very much as I have seen a mad old woman do upon the Dublin quays, and sometimes detect myself speaking and moving as if I were still young, or walking perhaps like an old man with fumbling steps. Occasionally I write out what I have said in verse, and generally for no better reason than because I remember that I have written no verse for a long time.

The self-consciousness of this little scene is very different from the unselfconscious Wordsworth making his turns on the gravel path. There is something roguish in the passage, a studied, throwaway effect—the impetus behind the writing, for example, being put down casually to the fact that the poet happens to remember that another lyric is due about now. Nevertheless, we feel that Yeats's account of himself acting out the poem's origin, turning the *donné* into display, is proper to the Yeatsian posture. Yeats does not listen in but acts out. The origin of the poetry is not a matter of sinking in but of coming up against, the mature music is not a lulling but an alerting strain. Padraic Colum once spoke of Yeats's poems having to be handled as carefully as a blade, and the image reminds us of Yeats's own ambitions for the work, poems 'the poet sings them with such airs/That one believes he has a sword upstairs'; poems 'cold and passionate as the dawn'; plays where he hopes 'the passion of the verse comes from the fact that the speakers are holding down violence or madness—down, hysterica passio. All depends on the completeness of the holding down, on the stirring of the beast underneath.' It is just such a note we hear in the major poems, as in 'The Tower':

> Now shall I make my soul,
> Compelling it to study
> In a learned school
> Till the wreck of body,
> Slow decay of blood,
> Testy delirium
> Or dull decrepitude,
> Or what worst evil come—
> The death of friends, or death

> Of every brilliant eye
> That made a catch in the breath—
> Seem but the clouds of the sky
> When the horizon fades,
> Or a bird's sleepy cry
> Among the deepening shades.

This is theatrical in its triumph, and many of the high moments in the *Collected Poems* share its rhetorical cast. At its worst that rhetoric is bragging; at its level best it has, to use Denis Donoghue's finely tuned adjective, an equestrian authority, which arises from Yeats's certainty that 'all the old writers, the masculine writers of the world, wrote to be spoken or to be sung, and in a later age to be read aloud for hearers who had to understand swiftly or not at all.' This Yeats who declared himself impatient with 'poetical literature, that is effeminate in its continual insistence upon certain moments of strained lyricism', sought a music that came ringing back off the ear as barely and resonantly as a shout caught back off a pillar in an empty church. It is indeed the music of energy reined down, of the mastered beast stirring:

> A sudden blow: the great wings beating still
> Above the staggering girl, her thighs caressed
> By the dark webs, her nape caught in his bill,
> He holds her helpless breast upon his breast . . .

> Turning and turning in the widening gyre
> The falcon cannot hear the falconer;
> Things fall apart; the centre cannot hold;
> Mere anarchy is loosed upon the world,
> The blood-dimmed tide is loosed, and everywhere
> The ceremony of innocence is drowned . . .

> Grant me an old man's frenzy,
> Myself must I remake
> Till I am Timon and Lear
> Or that William Blake
> Who beat upon the wall
> Till Truth obeyed his call . . .

In Yeats, the voice muscles its way over the obstacle course of the form and flexes like an animated vine on the trellis of its

73

metric and rhyme scheme. We are aware of the finished poem as an impressive thing in itself but somehow more impressive because of a threshold of difficulties now overcome. Those difficulties, of course, he exulted in: 'The Fascination of What's Difficult' complains of more things than the toil of artistic creation, but its rebounding utterance is won out of that central struggle:

> The fascination of what's difficult
> Has dried the sap out of my veins, and rent
> Spontaneous joy and natural content
> Out of my heart. There's something ails our colt
> That must, as if it had not holy blood
> Nor on Olympus leaped from cloud to cloud,
> Shiver under the lash, strain, sweat and jolt
> As though it dragged road-metal. My curse on plays
> That have to be set up in fifty ways,
> On the day's war with every knave and dolt,
> Theatre business, management of men.
> I swear before the dawn comes round again
> I'll find the stable and pull out the bolt.

The words fly off there like stones in a riot; this is not a region to wander in but a combat zone where rhymes collide and assertions strike hard music off one another like quarter-staffs striking. 'My curse on plays/That have to be set up in fifty ways'—yet it is one of Yeats's remarks, in *Explorations*, about the revision of his plays which throws light upon an important element in the makings of his music:

I have written a good many plays in verse and prose and almost all those plays I have re-written after performance, sometimes again and again, and every re-writing that has succeeded upon the stage has been an addition to the masculine element, an increase in the bony structure.

We can see how the bony structure has grown in this instance when we compare the sonnet with the first jottings in Yeats's notebook:

Subject To complain of the fascination of what's difficult. It spoils spontaneity and pleasure, and wastes time. Repeat line ending difficult and rhyme on bolt, exalt, colt, jolt. One could use the thought that the winged and broken colt must drag a cart of stones

74

out of pride because it is difficult and end by denouncing drama, accounts, public contests, all that is merely difficult.

For Yeats, composition was no recollection in tranquillity, not a delivery of the dark embryo, but a mastery, a handling, a struggle towards maximum articulation. Paradoxically, one can employ George Bernard Shaw's dictum on style—'Effectiveness of assertion is the alpha and omega of style'—to suggest the direction and endeavour of Yeats's writing. Paradoxically, because Shaw's arguing voice was anathema to the young poet who was to write later in *Autobiographies* that Shaw discovered it was possible 'to write with great effect without music, without style either good or bad, to eliminate from the mind all emotional implication and prefer plain water to every vintage'. Yet it is this virtue of 'effectiveness of assertion' that is common to both.

There is a relation between the process of composition and the feel of the completed poem all through Yeats's work. From the beginning things had to be well made, the soul had to be compelled to study, the images had to be masterful:

> A line will take us hours maybe;
> Yet if it does not seem a moment's thought,
> Our stitching and unstitching has been naught.
> Better go down upon your marrow bones
> And scrub a kitchen pavement, or break stones
> Like an old pauper, in all kinds of weather;
> For to articulate sweet sounds together
> Is to work harder than all these . . .

Scrubbing pavements, breaking stones—these things are contrasted with the craft of verse only to partake of its nature in the context of the poem itself. The abrasive and unyielding are necessarily present in the creative encounter, the mill of the mind has its work to do, for, as the lady affirms a little later in 'Adam's Curse', 'we must labour to be beautiful'. Thoughts do not ooze out and into one another, they are hammered into unity. 'All reality', Yeats notes in a 'Diary Written in 1930', 'comes to us as the reward of labour.' And at the end of his life, in 'A General Introduction to my Work', the theme of labour and deliberate effort comes up again: 'I compel myself to use those traditional metres that have developed with the language.'

Yet even traditional metres had to be subdued to the Yeatsian element:

> It was a long time before I had made a language to my liking; I began to make it when I discovered some twenty years ago that I must seek, not as Wordsworth thought, words in common use, but a more powerful and passionate syntax, a complete coincidence between period and stanza.

The concern is for syntax the controller, the compelling element that binds the constituent elements of sense into active unity.

But it is not only in Yeats's writings about composition that this urge to mastery can be discovered. It becomes most obvious in his manuscripts, in the evidence there of relentless concentration and self-criticism, in the evolution of driving verse from metrical monotony and, in many cases, plain ugly sentences. It is clear that the unwavering ceremonious procedures of his verse depend upon the way he wrought strongly for finish in the act of composition itself. One is reminded of a phrase by that other 'masculine' talent, Gerard Manley Hopkins, who spoke of 'a strain of address'; and Hopkins also spoke of 'that feeling of physical constraint that I want'.

All this is relevant to the success of a poem like 'Death'. 'Death' does not depend upon the way words woo themselves; the consonantal music and the short line work against any collusion between the vowels, the consonants and line-breaks acting as forcing agents, ramrodding the climax rhyme by rhyme:

> Nor dread nor hope attend
> A dying animal;
> A man awaits his end
> Dreading and hoping all;
> Many times he died,
> Many times rose again.
> A great man in his pride
> Confronting murderous men
> Casts derision upon
> Supersession of breath;
> He knows death to the bone—
> Man has created death.

76

Again, it is that accumulating pressure in the movement, the sense of passion held down, that we are responding to. The poem's arch is built on repetitions that strain away from one another by reason of the sense they are making, but press in upon one another by reason of the repeated vocable. Dread, hope, man, many times, death—the weight of the utterance forces these words against themselves and the rhymes on died/ pride and breath/death form the unshakeable arch of the structure. Affirmation arises out of oppositions.

'Long-legged Fly' is a poem that is absolute in its poetic integrity, that commands us both by the stony clarity of its sounds and the deep probes of its images, though 'images' is too weak a word, is somehow inaccurate: it is more that every element in the poem is at once literal and symbolic. It is a transcendent realization of the things I was trying to get at: what is the relationship between the creative moment in the life of an individual and the effect of that moment's conception throughout history?

> That civilization may not sink,
> Its great battle lost,
> Quiet the dog, tether the pony
> To a distant post;
> Our master Caesar is in the tent
> Where the maps are spread,
> His eyes fixed upon nothing,
> A hand under his head.
> *Like a long-legged fly upon the stream*
> *His mind moves upon silence.*
>
> That the topless towers be burnt
> And men recall that face,
> Move most gently if move you must
> In this lonely place.
> She thinks, part woman, three parts a child
> That nobody looks; her feet
> Practise a tinker shuffle
> Picked up on a street.
> *Like a long-legged fly upon the stream*
> *Her mind moves upon silence.*
>
> That girls at puberty may find
> The first Adam in their thought,
> Shut the door of the Pope's chapel,

Keep those children out.
There on that scaffolding reclines
Michael Angelo.
With no more sound than the mice make
His hand moves to and fro.
Like a long-legged fly upon the stream
His mind moves upon silence.

The creative mind is astraddle silence. In my reading, the long-legged fly has a masculine gender and while there is a sense of incubation permeating the whole poem, there is also a sense of intent siring. The image recalls the first chapter of the Book of Genesis, where God the Father's mind moves upon chaos, and the image functions within the poem like the nerve of a thinking brain, a brain that concedes the clangour and objectivity of historical events, the remorselessness of action, the unstoppable flow of time. It concedes all this but simultaneously affirms the absoluteness of the moment of silence, the power of the mind's motion along and against the current of history. The poem dramatizes concentration brought to the point of consummation. The act of the mind, in Michael Angelo's case, exerts an almost glandular pressure on history and what conducts that pressure is the image in the beholder's eye. In a similar way, as I have tried to show, poetry depends for its continuing efficacy upon the play of sound not only in the ear of the reader but also in the ear of the writer.

The first Kenneth Allott Memorial Lecture given at
Liverpool University, January 1978

The Fire i' the Flint

Reflections on the Poetry of
Gerard Manley Hopkins

What I have to say about Gerard Manley Hopkins springs from the slightly predatory curiosity of a poet interested in the creative processes of another poet. I want to cross a couple of ideas about poetry on each other, and hinge them in such a way as to take hold of and take some measure of the Hopkins opus. I want to approach him from the circumference of his art rather than from the centre of himself.

My title is taken from a speech by the Poet in *Timon of Athens* where Shakespeare seems to be glossing the abundance and naturalness of his own art briefly and completely. The Poet has been murmuring to himself, composing on the tongue as Wordsworth and Yeats were prone to do years afterwards, to the consternation of Cumberland peasant and Coole Park houseguest alike, when the Painter, who is bringing a picture as a gift to Timon, addresses him:

> You are rapt, sir, in some work, some dedication
> To the great lord

to which the Poet replies:

> A thing slipp'd idly from me.
> Our poesy is as a gum which oozes
> From whence 'tis nourished: the fire i' the flint
> Shows not till it be struck; our gentle flame
> Provokes itself, and, like the current, flies
> Each bound it chafes.

Much could be said about this spawn of metaphor in which the four elements combine and coagulate by sleight of word, but I

79

want to look at just one aspect, implicit in the very quick of the word 'slipp'd', which acts like a tuning fork for the music and movement of the whole piece. 'A thing slipp'd idly from me'—the poem is apparently dismissed as something let go or let fall almost accidentally; there is an understated tone to the phrase, an understatement artists are prone to when speaking about a finished work in order to protect the work's mystery and their own. Yet while the tone protects this mystery, and the immediate sense of 'slipp'd' makes light of the poem, behind the immediate sense lies a whole range of meanings and associations which insist on the poem as something nevertheless momentous in its occasion if momentary in its occurrence. Slip, after all, has also to do with unleashing energy; with taking a cutting for planting; and (if one were to engage in special pleading) with the moment of arrival, words coming safely and fluently towards us out of the uncharted waters of the unconscious. All in all, what is accidental, energetic, and genetic in the poetic act is hinted at here in one syllable: the slipping is the slipping envisaged by Robert Frost when he declared that 'like a piece of ice on a hot stove the poem must ride on its own melting.' So the nonchalance of the Poet's tone is complicated by big—as in 'big with child'—implications in the word's ramifying meanings and associations. And it is these ramifications which begin to spread and net in the following lines:

> Our poesy is as a gum which oozes
> From whence 'tis nourished . . .

The slip has become the slip almost of mucus, the smoothness of the verse insinuating a sense of natural release, the intimations of propagation becoming explicit in the ooze and nurture of the gum tree. And later, when 'our gentle flame provokes itself', the stirrings of the flame are as involuntary as the sexual stirrings which initiate growth and life itself; in fact, the flame is something of an aura, the flicker at the edge of the ovum under the microscope, a totally different kind of incandescence from the frigid sparks out of stone with which it is explicitly contrasted because, unlike this organic, oozy marshlight,

> the fire i' the flint
> Shows not till it be struck.

You may now have begun to see my drift, but I want you to be patient while, like the current, I fly the bound I chafe. Or, to use a subsequent speech of the Poet's on his own procedures:

> my free drift
> Halts not particularly, but moves itself
> In a wide sea of wax—

a wax which I hope to mould before the end of the lecture.

The kind of poetry in the speech I have just considered—perhaps too particularly—is the kind of poetry which Eliot had in mind when he spoke of the auditory imagination, that feeling for word and syllable reaching down below the ordinary levels of language, uniting the primitive and civilized associations words have accrued. It is a poetry that offers a continuous invitation into its echoes and recesses:

> Light thickens
> And the crow makes wing to the rooky wood;
> Good things of day begin to droop and drowse . . .

It is the kind of poetry symbolists wrote at the end of the nineteenth century and poets with an aspiration towards symbolism required in the twentieth: 'A poem should be palpable and mute . . . wordless/as the flight of birds . . . A poem should not mean/but be'—the popularity of Archibald MacLeish's poem is striking evidence of how current this view of poetry became.

To put it another way, the function of language in much modern poetry, and in much poetry admired by moderns, is to talk about itself to itself. The poem is a complex word, a linguistic exploration whose tracks melt as it maps its own progress. Whether they are defining poetry or writing it, the sense of poetry as ineluctably itself and not some other thing persists for modern poets. Here is Wallace Stevens defining it, in 'Adagia':

> Poetry creates a fictitious existence on an exquisite plane. This definition must vary as the plane varies, an exquisite plane being merely illustrative.

And here is T. S. Eliot writing it, on an exquisite plane, in 'Marina':

Bowsprit cracked with ice and paint cracked with heat.
I made this, I have forgotten
And remember
Between one June and another September.
Made this unknown, half conscious, unknown, my own.
The garboard strake leaks, the seams need caulking.
This form, this face, this life
Living to live in a world of time beyond me; let me
Resign my life for this life, my speech for that unspoken,
The awakened, lips parted, the hope, the new ships.

Now while this drives from a situation in Shakespeare's *Pericles*, knowledge of the derivation does not limit but liberates the scope of the poetry. For here we have 'de la musique avant toute chose'. The ear has incubated a cadence, a cadence which is to be found in the epigraph to the poem itself and which may well have constituted, in Valéry's terms, the poem's *donné*:

> Quis hic locus, quae
> regio, quae mundi plaga?

Eliot himself has discussed all this in 'The Three Voices of Poetry' and C. K. Stead has followed the trail admirably in *The New Poetic*. The self conspires with the self and hatches not a plot but an image. The voice pays back into itself and argues nothing. 'It cannot be too strongly stated that a poem is not the expression of a feeling the poet had before he began to write', Laforgue insisted with a bored wink to Eliot who took the tip and affirmed:

> It is the poet's business to be original . . . only so far as is absolutely necessary for saying what he has to say; only so far as is dictated, not by the idea—for there is no idea—but by the nature of that dark embryo within him which gradually takes on the form and speech of a poem.

And again, in another context:

> He is going to all that trouble, not in order to communicate with anyone, but to gain relief from acute discomfort. And when the words are finally arranged in the right way . . . he may experience a moment of exhaustion, of appeasement, of absolution, and of something very near annihilation which is in itself indescribable.

The symbolist image of poetic creation, one might say, is the unburdening of the indefinable through pangs that are indescribable, where the poem survives as the hieroglyph of a numinous nativity. At any rate, from Shakespeare's ooze to Eliot's dark embryo, we have a vision of poetic creation as a feminine action, almost parthenogenetic, where it is the ovum and its potential rather than the sperm and its penetration that underlies their accounts of poetic origins. And out of this vision of feminine action comes a language for poetry that tends to brood and breed, crop and cluster, with a texture of echo and implication, trawling the pool of the ear with a net of associations.

To take one final well-known example of the kind of work I am thinking of:

O rose, thou art sick!
The invisible worm
That flies in the night,
In the howling storm,

Has found out thy bed
Of crimson joy:
And his dark secret love
Does thy life destroy.

These eight lines of Blake's are like four loaves and four fishes that shoal and crumble as we try to consume their meaning. A rose is a rose is a rose but not when it's sick. Then it becomes a canker, a corruption, a tainted cosmos. The poem drops petal after petal of suggestion without ever revealing its stripped core: it is an open invitation into its meaning rather than an assertion of it.

Now I wonder if we can say the same of this poem, also short, also living off the life of its images:

Heaven-Haven
A nun takes the veil

I have desired to go
Where springs not fail
To fields where flies no sharp and sided hail
And a few lilies blow.

83

> And I have asked to be
> Where no storms come,
> Where the green swell is in the havens dumb
> And out of the swing of the sea.

In each case the verse lives by its music and suggestiveness, but with one important difference: the suggestiveness here condenses on a stated theme, 'a nun takes the veil', and the heaven–purity–cold idea equates with the haven–nunnery–quiet images in a relationship that is essentially allegorical rather than symbolic. The Hopkins poem is fretted rather than fecund. In the Blake poem the rose might be a girl but it remains a rose. Yet it is also a rose window, bloodshot with the light of other possible meanings. The rose and the sickness are not illustrative in the way the lilies and the haven are. In 'Heaven-Haven' it is the way things are exquisitely wrought, the way a crystal is sharp and sided and knowable rather than the way a rose is deep and unknowable that counts. Hopkins's art here is the discovery of verbal equivalents, in mingling the purity of images with the idea of a vow of chastity. The words are crafted together more than they are coaxed out of one another, and they are crafted in the service of an idea that precedes the poem, is independent of it and to which the poem is perhaps ultimately subservient. So much for the dark embryo. We are now in the realm of flint-spark rather than marshlight. 'Heaven-Haven' is consonantal fire struck by idea off language. The current of its idea does not fly the bound it chafes but confines itself within delightful ornamental channels.

To take another comparison with a poet whose nervous apprehension of phenomena and ability to translate this nervous energy into phrases reminds us also of Hopkins: take this line by Keats, describing autumn as the season of fulfilment:

> Close bosom-friend of the maturing sun

and compare it with a Hopkins line that also realizes a sense of burgeoning and parturition, imagining Jesus in Mary's womb:

> Warm-laid grave of a womb-life grey.

Both lines rely on the amplitude of vowels for their dream of benign, blood-warm growth, but where Keats's vowels seem

like nubs, buds off a single *uh* or *oo*, yeasty growths that are
ready at any moment to relapse back into the original mother
sound, Hopkins's are defined, held apart, and in relation to one
another rather than in relation to the original nub: if they are
full they are also faceted. Hopkins's consonants alliterate to
maintain a design whereas Keats's release a flow. I am reminded
of something T. S. Eliot wrote comparing Shakespeare and Ben
Jonson. In Jonson, Eliot remarked in *The Sacred Wood*:

> unconscious does not respond to unconscious; no swarms of in-
> articulate feelings are aroused. The immediate appeal of Jonson is
> to the mind; his emotional tone is not in the single verse but in the
> design of the whole.

We must say much the same of the Keats and Hopkins lines.
Keats has the life of a swarm, fluent and merged; Hopkins has
the design of the honeycomb, definite and loaded. In Keats, the
rhythm is narcotic, in Hopkins it is a stimulant to the mind.
Keats woos us to receive, Hopkins alerts us to perceive.

I think that what is true of this single Hopkins line is
generally true of the kind of poetry he writes. For in spite of the
astounding richness of his music and the mimetic power of his
vocabulary, his use of language is disciplined by a philological
and rhetorical passion. There is a conscious push of the
deliberating intelligence, a siring strain rather than a birth-push
in his poetic act. Like Jonson, he is *poeta doctus*; like Jonson's,
his verse is 'rammed with life', butting ahead instead of hanging
back into its own centre. As opposed to the symbolist poetic, it
is concerned with statement instead of states of feeling. Indeed,
at this point it is interesting to recall Ben Jonson's strictures on
the Shakespearian fluency, rejecting linguistic mothering in
favour of rhetorical mastery. Jonson, you remember, was not
impressed by the way Shakespeare's current flies each bound it
chafes:

> I remember the players have often mentioned it as an honour to
> Shakespeare that in his writing, whatsoever he penned, he never
> blotted a line. My answer hath been, 'Would he had blotted a
> thousand.' ... He was, indeed, honest and of an open and free
> nature wherein he flowed with that facility that sometime it was
> necessary he should be stopped ... His wit was in his own power:
> would the rule of it had been so too.

Jonson believed that energy should not be slipped but kept leashed. He values control, rule, revision, how things are fit, how they are fitted. And the same is true of Hopkins: the rule of his own 'wit' was Hopkins's study both as priest and poet. He valued what he called 'the masculine powers' in poetry, the presence of 'powerful and active thought'—it was typical that when he realized his 'new rhythm' he had to schematize it into a metric. The following extracts from a letter to Coventry Patmore in which Hopkins discusses Keats are illuminating:

> It is impossible not to feel with weariness how his verse is at every turn abandoning itself to an unmanly and enervating luxury. It appears too that he said something like 'O for a life of impressions rather than thoughts' ... Nevertheless, I feel and see in him the beginnings of something opposite to this, of an interest in higher things, and of powerful and active thought ... His mind had, as it seems to me, the distinctly masculine powers in abundance, his character the manly virtues, but while he gave himself up to dreaming and self-indulgence, of course, they were in abeyance ... but ... his genius would have taken to an austere utterance in art. Reason, thought, what he did not want to live by, would have asserted itself presently.

As is so often the case when a poet is diagnosing the condition of another poet, Hopkins is here offering us something of a self-portrait. The development he divined for Keats was one which he had already undergone himself. For Hopkins, as a schoolboy and undergraduate, had aspired to the life of sensations rather than thoughts, had luxuriated poetically and had been touched by the gem-like flame of Walter Pater's influence at Oxford. His masculine powers of powerful and active thought were consciously developed, as consciously as his theories of sprung rhythm and his private language of instress and inscape: behind the one was a directed effort in Welsh and classical versification, behind the other a scholastic appetite for Scotism. We have only to look at his early poem 'A Vision of Mermaids' to realize that when he spoke of 'an unmanly and enervating luxury', he was speaking from experience.

> From their white waists a silver skirt was spread
> To mantle o'er the tail, such as is shed
> Around the Water Nymphs in fretted falls,
> At red Pompeii on medallion'd walls.

A tainted fin on either shoulder hung;
Their pansy-dark or bronzen locks were strung
With coral, shells, thick-pearlèd cords, whate'er
The abysmal Ocean hoards of strange and rare.

This is gum oozing from whence 'tis nourished all right, from that enervating, luxurious Keats whom the mature Hopkins rounded on. In spite of the felicity of 'pansy-dark' and the resonance of the fourth line, what we miss here is what Hopkins described in his own mature poetry:

> But as air, melody, is what strikes me most of all in music and design in painting, so design, pattern or what I am in the habit of calling 'inscape' is what above all I aim at in poetry.

In fact, he might have been speaking as his own ideal reader when he expressed his reaction to the music of Henry Purcell:

> It is the forgèd feature finds me; it is the rehearsal
> Of own, of abrúpt sélf there so thrusts on, so throngs the ear.

In this earliest work there is no sense of the poetic emotion distinguishing itself. His posture here is one of surrender to experience whereas in his maturer work it is one of mastery, of penetration. His own music thrusts and throngs and it is forged. It is the way words strike off one another, the way they are drilled, marched, and countermarched, rather than the way they philander and linger among themselves, that constitutes his proper music. Hopkins's sound and sense always aim to complement each other in a perfectly filled-in outline: his poems are closer to being verbal relief-work than to being a receding, imploding vortex of symbol.

I wish to make one final comparison with another poet in order to clarify this 'masculine' element in his approach. W. B. Yeats is also a poet in whom we are offered the arched back of English in place of its copious lap; and again in Yeats we are constantly aware of the intentness on structure, and the affirmative drive of thought running under the music, of which the music is the clear-tongued pealing. Like Hopkins, he was impatient of 'poetical literature, that is monotonous in its structure and effeminate in its insistence upon certain moments of strained lyricism' and he was possessed of 'the certainty that all the old writers, the masculine writers of the world, wrote to be spoken or to be sung, and in a later age to be read aloud for hearers who had to understand quickly or not at all.' These sentiments not only re-echo Hopkins's strictures upon Keats, but they also recall Hopkins's famous, impatient directions on how to get the best out of his work, for he too wrote to be spoken or to be sung: 'Take breath and read it with the ears, as I always wish to be read, and my verse becomes all right.' And in another context: 'Declaimed, the strange constructions would be dramatic and effective.' So I am setting up two modes and calling them masculine and feminine—but without the Victorian sexist overtones to be found in Hopkins's and Yeats's employment of the terms. In the masculine mode, the language functions as a form of address, of assertion or command, and the poetic effort has to do with conscious quelling and control of the materials, a labour of shaping; words are not music before they are anything else, nor are they drowsy from their slumber in the unconscious, but athletic, capable, displaying the muscle of sense. Whereas in the feminine mode the language functions more as evocation than as address, and the poetic effort is not so much a labour of design as it is an act of divination and revelation; words in the feminine mode behave with the lover's come-hither instead of the athlete's display, they constitute a poetry that is delicious as texture before it is recognized as architectonic.

Yet Hopkins's poetry is immediately appealing or repellent, depending on the reader's taste, just because of its texture: is its immediate appeal not to the nervous system? It has worked its passage as modern rather than Victorian poetry not because it was published in 1918 but because, as Geoffrey Hartmann has written in his introduction to his *Twentieth-Century Views* collection of essays:

> I. A. Richards, William Empson, and F. R. Leavis championed Hopkins as the classic example of the modern poet. They agreed that his strength was immediately bound up with the immediacy of his relation to words: he seemed to fulfil the dream that poetry was language speaking about itself, language uttering complex words that were meanings *as* words.

He seemed, in other words, to possess those characteristics that I have made typical of the feminine mode; yet I still believe that he is essentially closer to the masculine, rhetorical mode.

Let us take a celebrated example of Hopkins's modern imagist technique—taking imagist in Pound's sense of 'that which presents an intellectual and emotional complex in a moment of time'. This is the famous fourth stanza of 'The Wreck of the Deutschland' where the protagonist has emerged from the experience, at once terrible and renovating, of Christ's sudden irruption into his life:

> I am soft sift
> In an hourglass—at the wall
> Fast, but mined with a motion, a drift,
> And it crowds and it combs to the fall;
> I steady as a water in a well, to a poise, to a pane,
> But roped with, always, all the way down from the tall
> Fells or flanks of the voel, a vein
> Of the gospel proffer, a pressure, a principle, Christ's gift.

Here Hopkins's procedures and eccentricities almost insist on being appreciated. His interest in dialect and archaism, in the use of the Welsh 'voel', meaning a small hill; his tendency to invert the functions of parts of speech, making 'proffer' a noun instead of a verb; and his incredible precision in making the gospel a 'proffer', with its suggestion of urgency and obligation to accept, so much more alive than 'offer'—all of this invites comment. As does the fact that 'proffer' alliterates with 'pressure' and 'principle', three piston-strokes heightening the pressure down the line. Moreover, Hopkins's total possession of the silent contradictory motions of sand in the neck of an hourglass and water in the bowl of the hills, his completely exciting apprehension of these things in sound and sense allows one to comprehend easily what 'inscape' meant, and what he meant when he once wrote in his journal: 'I saw the inscape freshly, as if my eye were still growing.'

Now all this has the status of an imagist poem in its verbal life, but it has the status of analogy within the argument and structure of the whole poem. It works like this. The streaming of sand is faded into the downpour of streams on the fells or flanks of a hill, and what had been at the bottom a sinking becomes a source, because this downing motion from above sustains, and rises as, a spring. So that suddenly the downing motion of Christ, his dark descending, becomes not something to make the soul sink in a quicksand of terror but to steady and be sustained by descending graces—Hopkins could well cry here, 'See where Christ's blood streams in the firmament.' Once more, as in 'Heaven-Haven', but in a much more complex manner, the whole figurative life of the piece is analogous and diagrammatic; what is mimetic in the words is completely guaranteed by what is theological behind them, expressing the mystery of Christ's efficacy and action in human life:

> Thou art lightning and love, I found it, a winter and warm;
> Father and fondler of heart thou hast wrung:
> Hast thy dark descending and most art merciful then.

If one still needed convincing about how designed and intended all this was, how it lives not only in its linguistic elements but in the poet's pre-verbal intention and intellection, one might compare it with another stanza of linguistic virtuosity, of considerable imaginative force, written by another poet with a sacramental apprehension of the world. Dylan Thomas's lines in 'The Force That Through The Green Fuse Drives The Flower' also concern water and quicksand:

> The hand that swirls the water in the pool
> Stirs the quicksand; that ropes the blowing wind
> Hauls my shroud sail.
> And I am dumb to tell the hanging man
> How of my clay is made the hangman's lime.

This is much more the 'logic of imagination' than the 'logic of concepts', more the yeasty burgeoning of images from a dark embryo than the delighted and precise realization or incarnation of a mystery. It is not so much the word made flesh as the flesh made word. If we ask the question, whose hand swirls the quicksand, or who is the hanging man, we cannot and perhaps should not expect a precise answer. It is not that kind of poem. It is incantation, it deploys heraldic images—admittedly with excitement—but it does not aspire to spell an exact proposition. Whatever truth the poem proposes it is only co-extensive with the poem itself.

Whereas 'The Wreck of the Deutschland', of course, is the utterance of Hopkins's whole reality, of his myth, if you like,

and this reality or myth has been lived as the truth by generations before and since Hopkins. Yeats had to write his own holy
book, *A Vision*, before he could embody its truths in poems, and
those truths were finally 'a superhuman/Mirror-resembling
dream', the creation of a Romantic fiat. But Hopkins's holy
book was the New Testament, its commentary was the *Spiritual
Exercises* of St. Ignatius Loyola, its reality was in his own
experience of conversion and vocation to the Jesuit rule. His
intellect was not forced to choose between perfection of the life
or of the work but was compelled to bring them into congruence.

I wish to suggest that Hopkins did indeed embody this
congruence, that his understanding of the Christian mystery
and the poetic mystery were structured in the same way; and in
this respect, a remark by Ted Hughes in his Afterword to
A Choice of Shakespeare's Verse is very pertinent. Hughes
writes:

> Poetic imagination is determined finally by the state of negotia-
> tion—in a person or in a people—between man and his idea of the
> Creator. This is natural enough, and everything else is naturally
> enough subordinate to it. How things are between man and his idea
> of the Divinity determines everything in his life, the quality and
> connectedness of every feeling and thought, and the meaning of
> every action.

Whether or not this holds generally, it is particularly true of
Hopkins. His journals are scrupulous and slightly shocking
evidence of the way his imagination was in constant, almost
neurotic negotiation with his idea of the Creator, as on 24
September 1870 when he saw the Northern Lights and in the
entry immediately following that:

> At first I thought of silvery cloud until I saw that these were more
> luminous and did not dim the clearness of the stars in the Bear ...
> This busy working of nature wholly independent of the earth and
> seeming to go on in a strain of time not reckoned by our reckoning
> of days and years but simpler and as if correcting the preoccupation
> of the world by being preoccupied with and appealing to and dated
> to the day of judgement was like a new witness to God and filled me
> with delightful fear.
> Oct 20—Laus Deo—the river to-day and yesterday.

91

Again, the intimate negotiation was in progress—as abnega-
tion—the previous year, in the entry beginning under 24 January 1869:

> The elms have long been in red bloom and yesterday (the 11th) I
> saw small leaves on the brushwood at their roots. Some primroses
> out. But a penance which I was doing from Jan. 25 to July 25
> prevented my seeing much that half-year.

But perhaps the most succinct and celebrated intimacy is his
remark about the bluebell: 'I know the beauty of Our Lord by
it.'

His relationship with the idea of the Divinity not only determined the quality and connectedness of every feeling and
thought, but it underlay his poetic imagination and provided, in
Hughes's word, the groundplan of the poetic act as he conceived
it. For Hopkins, this act was closer to having fire struck from
him than it was to oozing gum; and the striking of flame, 'the
stroke dealt' from above is how he images God's intervention in
his life in 'The Wreck of the Deutschland'. God appears in the
opening stanza in powerful aspect, as much Thor as Jehovah,
ready to deal blows with his hammer:

> Thou mastering me
> God! Giver of breath and bread;
> World's strand, sway of the sea;
> Lord of living and dead;
> Thou hast bound bones and veins in me, fastened me flesh,
> And after it almost unmade, what with dread,
> Thy doing: and dost thou touch me afresh?
> Over again I feel thy finger and find thee.

This is a far more mature and demanding vision of the religious
vocation than that which we saw in 'Heaven-Haven': not quiet
retreat, not the religious life viewed from the outside but
uttered from the quick centre. The bronze notes of the verse
only serve to reinforce Hopkins's declaration to a bewildered
Bridges: 'What refers to myself in the poem is all strictly and
literally true and did all occur; nothing is added for poetical
padding.' It would be possible to read the first ten stanzas of the
poem and relate the poetic mode, the psychological states, and
the theological implications line by line, but I will confine

myself to quotation and commentary relevant to my particular purpose.

Christ's storming of the soul is presented in images of lightning and fire:

> I did say yes
> O at lightning and lashed rod:
>
> .   .   .   .
>
> And the midriff astrain with leaning of, laced with fire of stress.

It is as if the 'sweep and hurl' fanned him into a glow, a glow which ignites his heart into a leaping flame of recognition and love:

> My heart, but you were dovewinged, I can tell,
>   Carrier-witted, I am bold to boast
> To flash from the flame to the flame then, tower from the grace to
>   the grace.

After this refining fire, he is soft sift that steadies and is sustained by the gospel proffer. He perceives Christ instressed in creation and stresses Christ's reality by imitation: stanzas 5, 6, 7 and 8 are an orthodox meditation on and affirmation of the mystery of Christ's incarnation, its redemptive effect on all nature and the consequent sacramental efficacy of natural phenomena. Then in stanza 8 he returns to the moment of personal crisis, the realization of Christ in his own life, when 'the stress felt', 'the stroke dealt' bursts like a sloe on the tongue, 'brim, in a flash, full'. And there follows the clearest statement of the paradox of the religious vocation, of the Christian relationship with a master who demands all obedience from his creature in order that the creature may be perfectly himself:

> Thou art lightning and love, I found it, a winter and warm;
>   Father and fondler of heart thou hast wrung:
> Hast thy dark descending and most art merciful then.
>
>   With an anvil-ding
>   And with fire in him forge thy will
>   Or rather, rather then, stealing as Spring
>   Through him, melt him but master him still.

This act of mastery is an act of love: the creature was 'trod' and now he is 'melted but mastered'. A sceptical critic might be forgiven, indeed, for thinking of Yeats's 'Leda and the Swan' rather than George Herbert's 'The Collar'.

But what I want to note is the striking correspondence between the imagery used to describe this central event in Hopkins's religious life and the central action in his life as a poet, that is, the experience of the poetic act itself. In each case a bolt from the blue, a fire that strikes, a masculine touch, initiates the action. The sonnet 'To R.B.' is worth quoting in full:

> The fine delight that fathers thought; the strong
> Spur, live and lancing like the blowpipe flame,
> Breathes once and, quenchèd faster than it came,
> Leaves yet the mind a mother of immortal song.
>
> Nine months she then, nay years, nine years she long
> Within her wears, bears, cares and combs the same:
> The widow of an insight lost she lives, with aim
> Now known and hand at work now never wrong.
>
> Sweet fire the sire of muse, my soul needs this;
> I want the one rapture of an inspiration.
> O then if in my lagging lines you miss
>
> The roll, the rise, the carol, the creation,
> My winter world, that scarcely breathes that bliss
> Now, yields you, with some sighs, our explanation.

Obviously Hopkins cannot escape, in this figure, the mothering function of his imagination, but what is important is that this is not in his case parthenogenetic but comes about through the union of distinct sexual elements, and the crucial element is the penetrative, masculine spur of flame, 'sweet fire the sire of muse'. The mastering God who came with lightning and lashed rod and 'the strong/Spur, live and lancing like the blowpipe flame', partake of the same nature. The fire in his heart only shows when it is struck.

There can be no more explicit illustration of the interconnectedness of Hopkins's poetic and religious vocations than his account of the origins of 'The Wreck of the Deutschland'. The passage from his letter to R. W. Dixon in October 1878 is well known but worth recalling at some length:

You ask, do I write verse myself. What I had written I burnt before I became a Jesuit and resolved to write no more, as not belonging to my profession, unless it were by the wish of my superiors; so for seven years I wrote nothing but two or three little presentation pieces which occasion called for. But when in the winter of '75 the Deutschland was wrecked in the mouth of the Thames and five Franciscan nuns, exiles from Germany, aboard of her were drowned I was affected by the account and happening to say so to my rector he said that he wished someone would write a poem on the subject. On this hint I set to work and, though my hand was out at first, produced one. I had long had haunting my ear the echo of a new rhythm which now I realized on paper. . . . After writing this I held myself free to compose but cannot find it in my conscience to spend time upon it; so I have done little and shall do less.

Composition, in other words, was not just a matter of natural volition and personal appeasement but had to be a compliance with and an enactment of the will of God, and the will of God was the rule of his order, and the rule of his wit, in Jonson's term, was as much in the mastering grip of his rector as it was in the grip of his rhetoric. So much is explicit here, but implicit is the siring figure we find in his sonnet to Bridges. The new rhythm that was haunting his ear had the status of dark embryo, but it needed to be penetrated, fertilized by the dark descending will; the rector's suggestion had the status of an annunciation in what Stephen Dedalus, that other scholastic artist, called 'the virgin womb of the imagination'.

Moreover, since Hopkins's poems were conceived as the crossing of masculine strain on feminine potential, it is natural that they are most fully achieved when siring vision is most rapturously united with a sensuous apprehension of natural life. United, and not simply in attendance upon each other. The sonnet 'Spring', for example, while being a delightful piece of inscaping, with its

thrush

> Through the echoing timber does so rinse and wring
> The ear, it strikes like lightnings to hear him sing,

is nevertheless structurally a broken arch, with an octave of description aspiring towards a conjunction with a sestet of doctrine. Doctrine and description only hold hands, as it were, in 'Spring' but in 'The Windhover' they are in intense communion, the spirit holding intercourse (the Wordsworthian locution is entirely appropriate) with beauty. In fact, 'The Windhover' is an extended mime of the process described in the sonnet to Bridges, an anatomy of the moment of inspiration and illumination, when the blowpipe flame of delight and insight lances the sensibility:

> I caught this morning morning's minion, king-
> dom of daylight's dauphin, dapple-dawn-drawn Falcon, in his
> riding
> Of the rolling level underneath him steady air, and striding
> High there, how he rung upon the rein of a wimpling wing
> In his ecstasy!

The octave of the sonnet constitutes 'the fine delight that fathers thought' and the thought is delivered in the moment of appeasement—'the achieve of, the mastery of the thing'. There follows the much interpreted sestet where Hopkins's imagination is luminously determined by his idea of the Creator, 'with aim/Now known and hand at work now never wrong'. Human perfection in the Christian sphere is not just a matter of dealing out physical being, or of flashing 'honour . . . off exploit', as in the case of the animal and secular worlds: all the panoply of such mastery must be downed when Christ is master, must buckle under the 'anvil ding' and be tempered to a new brilliance. The final lines do indeed vault into the consciousness with the lift of symbol, and yet, despite the gleam and deliquescence and intense sufficiency of the verbal art, they are still intent on telling a truth independent of themselves, that the fire in the flint of nature shows not till it be struck, and that nature's 'bonniest . . . her clearest selvèd spark/Man' is only completely selved and achieved in a selfless imitation of Christ. And this conclusion is not rhetoric in the pejorative sense, not the will doing the work of the imagination: not a mustered hurrah for asceticism in face of full-blooded exultation, but a whole man's 'wincing and singing':

> No wonder of it: shéer plód makes plough down sillion
> Shine, and blue-bleak embers, ah my dear,
> Fall, gall themselves, and gash gold-vermillion.

When I settled on 'the fire i' the flint' as the dark embryo for what I have been developing here, I wanted to explore the notion that the artist's idea of the artistic act, conscious or unconscious, affected certain intrinsic qualities of the artefact. I hope I have clarified my sense of the artistic act in Hopkins as a masculine forging rather than a feminine incubation, with a consequent intentness rather than allure in his style. His idea of the Creator himself as father and fondler is central to the mastering, design-making rhetoric and fondling of detail in his work. And just as Christ's mastering descent into the soul is an act of love, a treading and a melting, so the poetic act itself is a love-act initiated by the masculine spur of delight. But Hopkins was no doubt aware that even the act of love could be read as a faithful imitation of Christ, a sign of grace, insofar as the Church fathers perceived the sign of the cross in the figure of a man and woman splayed.

The Chatterton Lecture on an English Poet given at the British Academy, December 1974

Yeats as an Example?

A writer's dedication to his art can often entail some kind of hurt for those who live near and dear to him. Robert Lowell in the final poem of *The Dolphin* used the word 'plotting' to describe something that is questionable in the artistic enterprise:

> I have sat and listened to too many
> words of the collaborating muse,
> and plotted perhaps too freely with my life,
> not avoiding injury to others,
> not avoiding injury to myself—
> to ask compassion . . . this book, half-fiction,
> an eelnet made by man for the eel fighting—
>
> my eyes have seen what my hand did.

If there is more than a hint of self-accusation in that last line, there is a strong ring of triumph in it as well, and when Robert Lowell died I remember some of us toyed with it as a possible epitaph for him: it seemed to catch the combination of pride and vulnerability that lay at the roots of his poetic voice.

It would have made a much more rueful tombstone verse than Yeats's:

> Cast a cold eye
> On life, on death.
> Horseman, pass by.

Where Yeats's eye is cold, Lowell's is warm though by no means wet, sympathetic to the imperfections of living, the eye of a pedestrian rather than the eye of an equestrian. Where Yeats's last poems sang their faith in art and turned in scorn from 'the sort now growing up', Lowell's final work hesitated, and his trust in fictions seemed to waver:

Epilogue

Those blessed structures, plot and rhyme—
why are they no help to me now
I want to make
something imagined, not recalled? . . .

Yet why not say what happened?
Pray for the grace of accuracy
Vermeer gave to the sun's illumination
stealing like the tide across a map
to his girl solid with yearning.
We are poor passing facts,
warned by that to give
each figure in the photograph
his living name.

'Accuracy' seems a modest aim, even when it is as richly managed as it is here. Lowell abjures the sublime, that realm where his rhetoric often penetrated, and seeks instead the low-key consolations of the quotidian. He is almost, in Yeats's words, 'content to live'.

Yeats would never have been 'content to live' merely, because that would have meant throwing words away, throwing gesture away, throwing away possibilities for drama and transcendence. From the beginning of his career he emphasized and realized the otherness of art from life, dream from action, and by the end he moved within his mode of vision as within some invisible ring of influence and defence, some bullet-proof glass of the spirit, exclusive as Caesar in his tent, absorbed as a long-legged fly on the stream.

Whatever Yeats intends us to understand by 'Long-legged Fly', we cannot miss the confidence that drives it forward and the energy that underlies it, an energy that exhilarates in the faith that artistic process has some kind of absolute validity. There is a kind of vitreous finish on the work itself that deflects all other truths except its own. Art can outface history, the imagination can disdain happenings once it has incubated and mastered the secret behind happenings. In fact, we can sense a violence, an implacable element in the artistic drive as Yeats envisages and embodies it. The 'yellow eyed hawk of the mind' and the 'ancient, glittering eyes' of the Chinamen in 'Lapis

99

Lazuli' and the 'cold eye' of the tomb-inspecting horseman are all suggestive of sinister appetites. If the act of mind in the artist has all the intentness and amorousness and every bit as much of the submerged aggression of the act of love, then it can be maintained that Yeats's artistic imagination was often in a condition that only be properly described as priapic.

Is this, then, exemplary? Do we altogether assent to the samurai stare and certainty of 'Cast a cold eye/On life, on death'? Do we say yes to this high-stepping tread? Can we afford to disdain the life that goes on messily and cantankerously? How, in other words, do we regard Yeats's affirmation that the man who sits down to breakfast is a 'bundle of accident and incoherence' and that the man reborn in his poem is 'something intended, complete'?

Personally, I find much to admire in the intransigence of the stance, as I find much to commend and imitate in the two things that Yeats was so often determined to set at loggerheads, his life and his work:

> The intellect of man is forced to choose
> Perfection of the life or of the work
> And if it take the second must refuse
> A heavenly mansion, raging in the dark.

What is finally admirable is the way his life and his work are *not* separate but make a continuum, the way the courage of his vision did not confine itself to rhetorics but issued in actions. Unlike Wallace Stevens, for example, that other great apologist of the imagination, Yeats bore the implications of his romanticism into action: he propagandized, speechified, fund-raised, administered and politicked in the world of telegrams and anger, all on behalf of the world of vision. His poetry was not just a matter of printed books making their way in a world of literate readers and critics; it was rather the fine flower of his efforts to live as forthrightly as he could in the world of illiterates and politicians. Beside the ringing antithesis of 'The Choice' we must set this other recognition:

> A poet is by the very nature of things a man who lives with entire sincerity, or rather, the better his poetry, the more sincere his life. His life is an experiment in living and those who come after him have a right to know it. Above all, it is necessary that the lyric poet's life be known, that we should understand that his poetry is no

100

rootless flower but the speech of a man; that it is no little thing to achieve anything in any art, to stand alone perhaps for many years, to go a path no other man has gone, to accept one's own thought when the thought of others has the authority of the world behind it ... to give one's own life as well as one's words (which are so much nearer to one's soul) to the criticism of the world.

I admire the way that Yeats took on the world on his own terms, defined the areas where he would negotiate and where he would not; the way he never accepted the terms of another's argument but propounded his own. I assume that this peremptoriness, this apparent arrogance, is exemplary in an artist, that it is proper and even necessary for him to insist on his own language, his own vision, his own terms of reference. This will often seem like irresponsibility or affectation, sometimes like callousness, but from the artist's point of view it is an act of integrity, or an act of cunning to protect the integrity.

All through his life, of course, and ever since his death, Yeats has been continually rebuked for the waywardness of his beliefs, the remoteness of his behaviour and the eccentricity of his terms of reference. Fairies first of all. Then Renaissance courts in Tuscany and Big Houses in Galway. Then Phases of the Moon and Great Wheels. What, says the reliable citizen, is the sense of all this? Why do we listen to this gullible aesthete rehearsing the delusions of an illiterate peasantry, this snobbish hanger-on in country houses mystifying the feudal facts of the class system, this charlatan patterning history and predicting the future by a mumbo-jumbo of geometry and Ptolomaic astronomy? Our temptation may be to answer on the reliable citizen's terms, let him call the tune and begin to make excuses for Yeats.

'Well,' we might say, 'when he was a youngster in Sligo he heard these stories about fairies from the servants in his grand-parents' house; and then when, as a young poet, he sought a badge of identity for his own culture, something that would mark it off from the rest of the English-speaking world, he found this distinctive and sympathetic thing in the magical world view of the country people. It was a conscious counter-culture act against the rationalism and materialism of late Victorian England.' To which the citizen replies, 'Anybody who believes in fairies is mad.'

Yeats would not have thanked us for explaining him apologetically. He would want us to affirm him with all the elaborate obstinacy with which he affirmed himself. So for entertainment and instruction, I wish to observe him in action as a young poet, and then as an established poet and public figure; and in each case I hope to make clear what I consider to have been exemplary in his bearing.

The *Irish Theosophist*, a magazine whose very title is enough to raise the ghosts of the nineties, carried an interview with Mr. W. B. Yeats in its issue for 15 October 1893. It had been conducted by the editor, one D. N. Dunlop, who set the scene in his opening paragraphs:

> A few evenings ago I called on my friend, Mr. W. B. Yeats, and found him alone, seated in his armchair, smoking his cigarette, with a volume of Homer before him. The whole room indicated the style and taste peculiar to its presiding genius. Upon the walls hung various designs by Blake and other less well-known symbolic artists; everywhere books and papers in apparently endless confusion.
>
> In his usual genial way he invited me to have a cup of tea with him. During this pleasant ceremony little was said, but sufficient to impress me more than ever with the fact that my host was supremely an artist, much in love with his art.

Yeats was then twenty-eight, and could deploy that elaborate style he had learned from Pater with as much indolent calculation on a sofa as in a sentence. If he had not yet formulated his theory of the mask, he had an instinctive grasp of the potency of his image; and if he does not altogether ruffle here in a manly pose, there is nevertheless a bit of a peacock display going on. The Homer volume was a good touch, and so was the cigarette and the 'ceremony' of the tea.

The young man whose concern for appearances had led him, a few years earlier, to ink his heels in order to disguise the holes in his socks had obviously mastered more complex and sure-footed strategies for holding the line between himself and the world around him. He had not, to be sure, acquired the peremptory authority which Frank O'Connor was to see in action decades later, when the poet could silence an argument or buttress a proposition with a remark such as 'Ah, but that was before the peacock screamed', but he had about him already a definite atmosphere, a style that declared allegiance to disciplines and sources of strength not shared by his contemporaries. He was an artist, devoted to the beautiful; he was a magician, adept among hidden powers; he was a Celt, with a lifeline to the mythological depths; he was a propagandist, with a firm line for journalists. He was all these things, self-consciously and deliberately, yet they did not constitute a dispersal or a confusion of his powers or of his personality; on the contrary, they concentrated one another, grew from a single root, and if they were deliberate, the deliberation sprang from an inner compulsion, an energy discovering itself as vision. Yeats's performances, we might say, then and for the rest of his life, manifested themselves in the service of creative action. The longer we think of Yeats, the more he narrows the gap which etymology has forced between mystery and mastery.

Aspects of the mysterious and the masterful reveal themselves in one of his coolest strokes during the interview, which was essentially a conversation about Yeats's connection with the Blavatsky Lodge of the Theosophical Society. He had been expelled by Madame Blavatsky, or at least had been asked to resign about three years earlier. Dunlop asked him:

'Can you remember anything in the nature of a prophecy, Mr. Yeats, made by Madame Blavatsky, that might be of interest to record, notwithstanding the fact that you are yet awaiting your prophesied illness?'

'The only thing of that nature,' replied Mr. Yeats, 'was a reference to England'. '"The Master told me," said she, "that the power of England would not outlast the century, and the Master never deceived me."'

It seems to me that Yeats cut a sly swathe with that answer, enlisting the esoteric fringe to serve the nationalistic heartland, hiding the cultural agitator behind the po-faced dreamer, making a cast across the sleeping pool of historical enmity with a line as neutral as theosophy itself, the calm surface of his speech depth-charged with potential rebellion. The remark leaves a broadening wake in the imagination and operates by the perfect camouflaging of judged intention in an aftermath of overlapping effects; and in this way it rehearses in miniature the more complex orchestration of intention and effect which he was to achieve in *The Wind Among the Reeds*, a book whose title was already haunting his mind.

'And what about your present work?' I asked.

'*Celtic Twilight*, a work dealing with ghosts, goblins and fairies, will be out shortly, also a short volume of Blake's poems,' he replied. 'Then I am getting ready for publication, next spring, a book of poems, which I intend calling *The Wind Among the Reeds* and, as soon afterwards as possible, a collection of essays and lectures dealing with Irish nationality and literature, which will probably appear under the title of the *Watch Fire*.'

In the event *Watch Fire* was never published. His essay on nationality and literature had appeared, however, five months earlier in the *United Irishman* and work on similar themes had been published all through the late eighties and continued to be published throughout the nineties. He began with his famous championship of Sir Samuel Ferguson's poetry—'the greatest poet Ireland has produced, because the most central and most Celtic'—and went on to praise James Clarence Mangan, William Allingham and the ballad poets; to sponsor new voices like Katherine Tynan's and AE's; to write for English and Irish magazines bibliographies and reader's guides to the best Irish books; to affirm the validity of that magical world-view implicit in Irish country customs and beliefs, and to rehearse those beliefs and customs in the book he mentions which gave its name to an era, *The Celtic Twilight*.

It was all part of a campaign and the various suggestions in the word campaign are apposite. It was sustained over a long period and was pursued on a number of fronts: journalistic, political, poetic, dramatic, amatory even, if we think of Maud Gonne as leading lady in *The Countess Cathleen*; it was pursued with the idea of conquest, not of territory perhaps but of imagination—though a successful awakening of the people's imagination would allow them to repossess their territory with a new conviction. As he comes to the end of that part of his autobiography dealing with the years 1887–1891, the note swells as he recollects his purpose:

I could not endure, however, an international art, picking stories and symbols where it pleased. Might I not, with health and good

104

luck to aid me, create some new *Prometheus Unbound*; Patrick or Colmcille, Oisin or Finn in Prometheus's stead; and, instead of Caucasus, Cro-Patrick or Ben Bulben? Have not all races had their first unity from a mythology that marries them to rock and hill? We had in Ireland imaginative stories, which the uneducated classes knew and even sang, and might we not make those stories current among the educated classes, rediscovering what I have called 'the applied arts of literature', the association of literature, that is, with music, speech and dance; and at last, it might be, so deepen the political passion of the nation that all, artist and poet, craftsman and day-labourer would accept a common design?

If there is something plangent in this proud recollection, there was nothing of the dying fall in the notes struck by the journalism and controversy of the eighties and nineties as he pursued that 'common design'. For example, after declaring in his 1886 *Dublin Magazine* article on Sir Samuel Ferguson that of all things the past bequeaths the future, the greatest are great legends and that it was therefore the duty of every Irish reader to study those of his own country, he went on to make clear that this appeal was directed to the selfless and idealistic young:

> I do not appeal to the professional classes, who, in Ireland, at least, appear at no time to have thought of the affairs of their country till they first feared for their emoluments—nor do I appeal to the shoddy society of 'West Britonism'....

That pugnacious thrust never deserted him, although he was to develop a less bare-fisted style, abandoning the short jab in the face in favour of a long reach for the side of the head.

The point is, however, that no matter how much we have been led to think of the young Yeats as a dreamer, we must not forget the practical, driving side of him, driving forward towards his ideal goal. The founding of libraries, the association with political activists, all this was not undertaken without some resoluteness, some ambition, some expense of spirit. And all of this was by no means the whole story. There were his love affairs, first with Maud Gonne and then with Olivia Shakespeare, those enhancing and disturbing events in his emotional life that gave him power in other spheres. There were his more serious literary projects, such as the stories of Red Hanrahan, and those other strange stories, at once robust and remote, which formed the substance of *The Secret Rose*; and there was above all his own secret rose, the poetry itself.

It is easy to admire this young Yeats: his artistic ambitions, his national fervour, his great desire to attach himself to a tradition and a corpus of belief that was communal. For all the activity and push of the enterprise, the aim of the poet and of the poetry is finally to be of service, to ply the effort of the individual work into the larger work of the community as a whole, and the spirit of our age is sympathetic to that democratic urge.

It is less than sympathetic, however, to the next stance we find the poet adopting. Twenty years after the *Irish Theosophist* interview in October 1893, in his poem 'September 1913', Yeats's style had evolved a tone for detaching rather than attaching himself, for saying 'I' rather than 'we'. By then, Romantic Ireland's dead and gone. We are in the presence of a poet in his late forties, the Abbey Theatre manager, scorner of middle-class piety and philistinism, mythologizer of aristocratic ceremony and grace. We are in the presence of a man who believes that the redistribution of the Coole Park estate among its tenants would be a step back, not a step forward, in the life of the country. A man stung into superb attitudes by the rude handling meted out to J. M. Synge's *Playboy of the Western World* and by the refusal of Dublin Corporation to provide a gallery for Hugh Lane's collection of Impressionist pictures. All that. An Anglo-Irish Protestant deeply at odds with the mind of Irish Catholic society. A man who is remaking himself, finding a style for resisting his environment rather than a style that would co-opt it, at that thrilling stage of development which he calls, in 'A Dialogue of Self and Soul', 'the finished man among his enemies'. And that poem goes on to ask about this man among his enemies:

> How in the name of heaven can he escape
> That defiling and disfiguring shape
> The mirror of malicious eyes
> Casts upon his eyes, until at last
> He thinks that shape must be his shape?

So I want our next image of Yeats to be one that the malicious eyes of George Moore cast into shape when he came to write his classic autobiographical account of the Irish Literary Revival in *Hail and Farewell*. Though 'malicious' is perhaps too severe an adjective. Many of Moore's most quotable jabs at the romantic figure of the poet are more suggestive of affection than of a desire to afflict, as when he describes his laugh as a caw, 'the most melancholy thing in the world', or when he presents a bedraggled Yeats on the margins of Coole Lake looking like an old umbrella left behind after a picnic. Moore's book is finally more of a testimony to Yeats's genius than a worrier of it, sustained and elaborate in its ironies, corrective, accurate in its own way. The following passage occurs after Moore has given his account of the Lane controversy and has reported the text of his own lecture on the Impressionists, a lecture delivered for the edification of the reluctant burghers:

> As soon as the applause died away, Yeats who had lately returned to us from the States with a paunch, a huge stride, and an immense fur overcoat, rose to speak. We were surprised at the change in his appearance, and could hardly believe our ears when, instead of talking to us as he used to do about the old stories come down from generation to generation he began to thunder like Ben Tillett against the middle classes, stamping his feet, working himself into a temper, and all because the middle classes did not dip their hands into their pockets and give Lane the money he wanted for his exhibition. When he spoke the words, the middle classes, one would have thought that he was speaking against a personal foe, and we looked round asking each other with our eyes where on earth our Willie Yeats had picked up the strange belief that none but titled and carriage-folk could appreciate pictures ...
>
> We have sacrificed our lives for Art; but you, what have you done? What sacrifices have you made? he asked, and everybody began to search his memory for the sacrifices that Yeats had made, asking himself in what prison Yeats had languished, what rags he had worn, what broken victuals he had eaten. As far as anybody could remember, he had always lived very comfortably, sitting down invariably to regular meals, and the old green cloak that was in keeping with his profession of romantic poet he had exchanged for the magnificent fur coat which distracted our attention from what he was saying, so opulently did it cover the back of the chair out of which he had risen ...

The conscious theatricality of this Yeats, the studied haughtiness, the affectation—this kind of thing has often put people off. This is the Willie Yeats whom his contemporaries could not altogether take seriously because he was getting out of their reach, the Yeats whom Maud Gonne called 'Silly Willie' and whom W. H. Auden also called 'silly', in his 1939 elegy: 'You were silly like us, your gift survived it all.' But in setting the silliness in relation to the gift, Auden went to the heart of the matter—survival. What Moore presents us with is a picture of Yeats exercising that intransigence which I praised earlier, that protectiveness of his imaginative springs, so that the gift would survive. He donned the mantle—or perhaps one should say the fur coat—of the aristocrat so that he might express a vision of a communal and personal life that was ample, generous, harmonious, fulfilled and enhancing. The reactionary politics implied by Yeats's admiration of the Coole Park milieu are innocent in the original sense of that word, not nocent, not hurtful. What is more to the point is the way his experience of that benign, paternalistic regime and of Lady Gregory's personal strengths as conserver of folk culture and choreographer of artistic talent issued in a poetry whose very music is a guarantee of its humane munificence. The silliness of the behaviour is continuous with the sumptuousness of the poetry of the middle period. Yeats's attack upon his own middle class really springs out of disappointment: why aren't they taking the lead culturally now that they are in the lead economically? Of course Moore is right to say he belongs to them, and of course Yeats's pretensions looked ridiculous to his contemporaries. But this was his method of signifying his refusal to 'serve that in which he no longer believed'.

When Joyce rebelled, he left by the Holyhead boat and created his drama by making a fictional character called Stephen Dedalus point up and repeat the terms of his revolt. When Yeats rebelled, he remained—Joyce scorned such 'a treacherous instinct for adaptability'—but he still made a new W. B. Yeats to tread the streets and stage of Dublin, a character who was almost as much a work of imagination as Stephen Dedalus. In order to fly the philistinism of his own class and the pious ignorance of another creed, Yeats remade himself, associated himself with cold, disdainful figures of whom Charles Stewart Parnell was the archetype and 'The Fisherman' was a pattern. The solitude, the will towards excellence, the courage, the self-conscious turning away from that in which he no longer believes, which is Dublin life, and turning towards that which he trusts, which is an image or dream—all the drama and integrity of his poem 'The Fisherman' depend to a large extent upon that other drama which George Moore so delightedly observed and reported:

> Maybe a twelvemonth since
> Suddenly I began,
> In scorn of this audience,
> Imagining a man,
> And his sun-freckled face,
> And grey Connemara cloth,
> Climbing up to a place
> Where stone is dark under froth,
> And the down-turn of his wrist
> When the flies drop in the stream;
> A man who does not exist,
> A man who is but a dream;
> And cried, 'Before I am old
> I shall have written him one
> Poem maybe as cold
> And passionate as the dawn.'

We are moving from what other people saw to what Yeats himself envisaged. I have said enough, I think, about the outer man and what he intended, so it is time to consider the inwardness of the poems instead of the outwardness of the stance.

Yet the poetry is cast in a form that is as ear-catching as the man was eye-catching, and as a writer, one is awed by the achieved and masterful tones of that deliberately pitched voice, its bare classic shapes, its ability to modulate from emotional climax to wise reflection, its ultimate truth to life. Nevertheless, the finally exemplary moments are those when this powerful artistic control is vulnerable to the pain or pathos of life itself.

But I have to say something about why I put the question-mark after the title of this lecture. 'Yeats as an Example' was the title of an appreciative but not ecstatic essay that W. H. Auden wrote in 1940, so my new punctuation is partly a way of referring back to Auden's title. But it is also meant to acknowledge the orthodox notion that a very great poet can be a very bad influence on other poets. What Yeats offers the practising

109

writer is an example of labour, perseverance. He is, indeed, the ideal example for a poet approaching middle age. He reminds you that revision and slog-work are what you may have to undergo if you seek the satisfactions of finish; he bothers you with the suggestion that if you have managed to do one kind of poem in your own way, you should cast off that way and face into another area of your experience until you have learned a new voice to say that area properly. He encourages you to experience a transfusion of energies from poetic forms themselves, reveals how the challenge of a metre can extend the resources of the voice. He proves that deliberation can be so intensified that it becomes synonymous with inspiration. Above all, he reminds you that art is intended, that is is part of the creative push of civilization itself: from 'Adam's Curse' to 'Vacillation' and on until the last poems, his work not only explicitly proclaims the reality of the poetic vocation but convinces by the deep note of certitude registered in the proclamation itself.

> No longer in Lethean foliage caught
> Begin the preparation for your death
> And from the fortieth winter by that thought
> Test every work of intellect or faith,
> And everything that your own hands have wrought,
> And call those works extravagance of breath
> That are not suited for such men as come
> Proud, open-eyed and laughing to the tomb.
>
> ('Vacillation')

> Malachi Stilt-Jack am I, whatever I learned has run wild,
> From collar to collar, from stilt to stilt, from father to child.
> All metaphor, Malachi, stilts and all. A barnacle goose
> Far up in the stretches of night; night splits and the dawn breaks
>   loose;
> I, through the terrible novelty of light, stalk on, stalk on;
> Those great sea-horses bare their teeth and laugh at the dawn.
>
> ('Malachi Stilt-Jack')

But it is not this vaunting of the special claims of art and the artist that is finally to be saluted. Rather, it is Yeats's large-minded, whole-hearted assent to the natural cycles of living and dying, his acknowledgement that the 'masterful images' which

110

compel the assent of artist and audience alike are dependent upon the 'foul rag-and-bone shop of the heart', the humility of his artistic mastery before the mystery of life and death. There are several poems where this tenderness towards life and its uncompletedness is at odds with and tending to gain sway over the consolations of the artificial work. The tumultuousness and repose of a poem like 'Sailing to Byzantium' comes to mind, although there the equilibrium between the golden bird of art and the tattered scarecrow of life is just held, as it is held and held in mind, contemplated and celebrated in 'Among School Children'. I am thinking, however, of quieter poems, more intimate, less deliberately orchestrated pieces, such as 'What Then?':

> All this happier dreams came true—
> A small old house, wife, daughter, son,
> Grounds where plum and cabbage grew,
> Poets and Wits about him drew;
> *'What then?' sang Plato's ghost. 'What then?'*
>
> 'The work is done,' grown old he thought,
> 'According to my boyish plan;
> Let the fools rage, I swerved in naught,
> Something to perfection brought';
> *But louder sang that ghost, 'What then?'*

And the challenge of Plato's ghost is matched and picked up in that other uncharacteristically introspective poem, 'The Man and the Echo', where the Echo mocks the Man and where the voice of conscience and remorse opposes itself to the artistic choice that the old man has lived out all his life; this voice of conscience which asks 'Did that play of mine send out/Certain men the English shot' is finally symbolized in the anguished cry of a rabbit:

> But hush for I have lost the theme,
> Its joy or might seem but a dream.
> Up there some hawk or owl has struck
> Dropping out of sky or rock,
> A stricken rabbit is crying out
> And its cry distracts my thought.

I want to finish with two poems, one of which sets the dissatisfied poet in the midst of civil war, the other of which sets the

111

violent hero in the middle of the dead. They ask, indirectly, about the purpose of art in the midst of life and by their movements, their images, their musics they make palpable a truth which Yeats was at first only able to affirm abstractly, in those words which he borrowed from Coventry Patmore: 'The end of art is peace.'

The first is from 'Meditations in Time of Civil War':

> The bees build in the crevices
> Of loosening masonry, and there
> The mother birds bring grubs and flies.
> My wall is loosening; honey-bees,
> Come build in the empty house of the stare.
>
> We are closed in, and the key is turned
> On our uncertainty; somewhere
> A man is killed, or a house burned,
> Yet no clear fact to be discerned:
> Come build in the empty house of the stare.
>
> A barricade of stone or of wood;
> Some fourteen days of civil war;
> Last night they trundled down the road
> That dead young soldier in his blood:
> Come build in the empty house of the stare.
>
> We had fed the heart on fantasies,
> The heart's grown brutal from the fare;
> More substance in our enmities
> Than in our love; O honey-bees,
> Come build in the empty house of the stare.

Here the great fur coat of attitude is laid aside, the domineering intellect and the equestrian profile, all of which gain him a power elsewhere, all laid aside. What we have is a deeply instinctive yet intellectually assented-to idea of nature in her benign and nurturant aspect as the proper first principle of life and living. The maternal is apprehended, intimated and warmly cherished and we are reminded, much as Shakespeare might remind us, of the warm eggs in the nest shaking at the impact of an explosion. The stare at Yeats's window and the temple-haunting martlet in Macbeth's castle are messengers of grace.

And if the maternal instincts are the first, perhaps they call us back at the very end also. Yeats lies under Ben Bulben, in Drumcliff Churchyard, under that dominant promontory which I like to think of as the father projected into the landscape, and there is perhaps something too male and assertive about the poem that bears the mountain's name and stands at the end of the *Collected Poems*. If I had my choice I would make the end of that book more exemplary by putting a kinder poem last, one in which the affirmative wilful violent man, whether he be artist or hero, the poet Yeats or the headhunter Cuchulain, must merge his domineering voice into the common voice of the living and the dead, mingle his heroism with the cowardice of his kind, lay his grey head upon the ashy breast of death.

I would end with 'Cuchulain Comforted', a poem which Yeats wrote within two weeks of his death, one in which his cunning as a deliberate maker and his wisdom as an intuitive thinker find a rich and strange conclusiveness. It is written in *terza rima*, the metre of Dante's *Commedia*, the only time Yeats used the form, but the proper time, when he was preparing his own death by imagining Cuchulain's descent among the shades. We witness here a strange ritual of surrender, a rite of passage from life into death, but a rite whose meaning is subsumed into song, into the otherness of art. It is a poem deeply at one with the weak and the strong of this earth, full of a motherly kindness towards life, but also unflinching in its belief in the propriety and beauty of life transcended into art, song, words. The language of the poem hallows the things of this world—eyes, branches, linen, shrouds, arms, needles, trees, all are strangely chaste in the context—yet the figure the poem makes is out of this world:

Cuchulain Comforted

A man that had six mortal wounds, a man
Violent and famous, strode among the dead;
Eyes stared out of the branches and were gone.

Then certain Shrouds that muttered head to head
Came and were gone. He leant upon a tree
As though to meditate on wounds and blood.

A Shroud that seemed to have authority
Among those bird-like things came, and let fall
A bundle of linen. Shrouds by two and three

Came creeping up because the man was still.
And thereupon that linen-carrier said:
'Your life can grow much sweeter if you will

'Obey our ancient rule and make a shroud;
Mainly because of what we only know
The rattle of those arms makes us afraid.

'We thread the needles' eyes, and all we do
All must together do.' That done, the man
Took up the nearest and began to sew.

'Now must we sing and sing the best we can,
But first you must be told our character:
Convicted cowards all, by kindred slain

'Or driven from home and left to die in fear.'
They sang, but had nor human tunes nor words,
Though all was done in common as before;

They had changed their throats and had the throats of birds.

Lecture given to General Studies Department,
University of Surrey, 1978

114

From Monaghan to the Grand Canal

The Poetry of Patrick Kavanagh

'I have never been much considered by the English critics'—
in the first sentence of Kavanagh's 'Author's Note' to the
Collected Poems (1964) it is hard to separate the bitterness
from the boldness of 'not caring'. It was written towards the
end of his career when he was sure, as I am, that he had
contributed originally and significantly to the Irish literary
tradition, not only in his poetry and his novel, *Tarry Flynn*
(1948), but also in his attempts to redefine the idea of that
tradition.

Matters of audience and tradition are important in discussing
Kavanagh. How do we 'place' him? It will not do to haul the
academic net and mention peasant poets like John Clare or
Stephen Duck. The poetry of these men is a bonus in an already
abundant poetic tradition; their achievements can be displayed
and cherished like corn dollies, adornments, lovely signals of
the total harvest. Their consciousness could hold on to the
rungs of established norms, there was a standard accent against
which their dialect could be evaluated. And if the English
parallels are unrewarding, it is almost equally difficult to posit
an Irish lineage. Kavanagh's proper idiom is free from the
intonations typical of the Revival poets. His imagination has not
been tutored to 'sweeten Ireland's wrong', his ear has not been
programmed to retrieve in English the lost music of verse in
Irish. The 'matter of Ireland', mythic, historical or literary,
forms no significant part of his material. There are a few
Yeatsian noises—'why should I lament the wind'—in *Plowman*
(1936), but in general the uncertain voice of that first book and
the authoritative voice of *The Great Hunger* (1942) cannot be

115

derived from the conventional notes of previous modern Irish poetry. What we have is something new, authentic and liberating. There is what I would call an artesian quality about his best work because for the first time since Brian Merriman's poetry in Irish at the end of the eighteenth century and William Carleton's novels in the nineteenth, a hard buried life that subsisted beyond the feel of middle-class novelists and romantic nationalist poets, a life denuded of 'folk' and picturesque elements, found its expression. And in expressing that life in *The Great Hunger* and in *Tarry Flynn* Kavanagh forged not so much a conscience as a consciousness for the great majority of his countrymen, crossing the pieties of a rural Catholic sensibility with the *non serviam* of his original personality, raising the inhibited energies of a subculture to the power of a cultural resource.

Much of his authority and oddity derive from the fact that he wrested his idiom bare-handed out of a literary nowhere. At its most expressive, his voice has the air of bursting a long battened-down silence. It comes on with news in the first line—'Clay is the word and clay is the flesh', 'I have lived in important places'—and it keeps on urgently and ebulliently to the last. It never settles itself into self-regard; it doesn't preen itself in felicities; it has a spoken rather than a written note— which means that when unsuccessful it sounds more like blather than bad verse—and it runs with a lovely jaunty confidence against its metrical norm. In his *Self Portrait* (1964) Kavanagh imagined himself jumping ditches with a load of white flour on his back, and this could be an image for the kind of risky buoyancy his best work achieves, a completely different kind of discipline from Austin Clarke's 'loading himself with golden chains and trying to escape'. Kavanagh is closer to the tightrope walker than the escape artist. There is, we might say, more technique than craft in his work, real technique which is, in his own words, 'a spiritual quality, a condition of mind, or an ability to invoke a particular condition of mind . . . a method of getting at life', but his technique has to be continuously renewed, as if previous achievements and failures added up to nothing in the way of self-knowledge or self-criticism of his own capacities as a maker. There is very little 'parnassian' in Kavanagh, very little sense of his deploying for a second time round technical discoveries originally made while delivering a poem of the first intensity out of its labour.

To begin, then, with the first such poem we meet in the *Collected Poems*, 'Inniskeen Road, July Evening':

> The bicycles go by in twos and threes—
> There's a dance in Billy Brennan's barn to-night,
> And there's a half-talk code of mysteries
> And the wink-and-elbow language of delight.
> Half-past eight and there is not a spot
> Upon a mile of road, no shadow thrown
> That might turn out a man or woman, not
> A footfall tapping secrecies of stone.
>
> I have what every poet hates in spite
> Of all the solemn talk of contemplation.
> O Alexander Selkirk knew the plight
> Of being king and government and nation.
> A road, a mile of kingdom, I am king
> Of banks and stones and every blooming thing.

The title names place and time, which is all-important in the world of early Kavanagh. Loved places are important places, and the right names 'snatch out of time the passionate transitory'. Inniskeen is the poet's birthplace where he lived on the family farm for more than thirty years, and it would seem that this poem comes towards the end of his sojourn for although it contemplates the scene in the present, there is a feeling of valediction about it. By the end, the experience has almost attained the status of memory, a regal distance intervenes, and impatience vies with affection in the ambiguous 'blooming'. The poet's stance becomes Wordsworth's over Tintern Abbey, attached by present feelings but conscious that the real value of the moment lies in its potential flowering, its blooming, in the imagination. Indeed, the poem could carry a Wordsworth subtitle, 'or, Solitude'.

There are two solitudes, the solitude of the road and the solitude of the poet, and the road's is an objective correlative of the poet's. The second quatrain has a curious double effect: the road has become still, there is neither sound nor shadow, and yet the negatives of 'no shadow thrown' and 'not a footfall' do not entirely rob the scene of its life. The power of the negated phrases, 'turn out a man or woman' and (especially) 'a footfall tapping secrecies of stone', works against the solitude and establishes a ghostly populous atmosphere, and this prepares us for the poet's double-edged feelings in the sestet of being at once marooned and in possession. I suppose the basic theme of the poem is the penalty of consciousness, the unease generated when a milieu becomes material. It is a love poem to a place written towards the end of the affair and it is also one of the earliest and most successful of Kavanagh's many poems about the nature of the poetic life. I have dwelt on it in some detail in order to show something that I believe even Kavanagh's admirers do not sufficiently realize, that he is a technician of considerable suppleness. I take great pleasure in that 'not' at the end of the seventh line, for example: the bag of flour has almost toppled him but that 'not' does not unbalance, it lands us instead on the lovely thawing floe of 'A footfall tapping secrecies of stone'.

Of course it would be wrong to insist too strongly on Kavanagh as a weaver of verbal textures. There is a feeling of prospector's luck—which may be deliberately achieved, but I don't think so—about many of his best effects. We need only compare the nice lift of a Kavanagh stanza with its inspired wobble, from 'A Christmas Childhood':

> Cassiopeia was over
> Cassidy's hanging hill,
> I looked and three whin bushes rode across
> The horizon—the Three Wise Kings

with lines by a wordsmith like Hopkins:

> Look at the stars! look, look up at the skies!
> O look at all the fire-folk sitting in the air!

to see that the attitudes towards form and language are completely different. Hopkins is a maker, Kavanagh a taker of verses, a grabber of them. He is not so much interested in the inscape of things as in their instress. He is, as it were, the Van Gogh rather than the Cézanne of Monaghan. The 'ineluctible modality of the visible' does not seek to transpose itself into aural or verbal patterning. The poem is more a conductor than a crucible. It seeks 'weightlessness'—a quality he praised in one

of his own stanzas—rather than density: which is not to say that
it abjures the concrete. On the contrary, the poetry is most
successful when it is earthed in the actual where 'the light that
might be mystic or a fraud' can strike and be contained.

Which brings us back to *Plowman*. I have seen this book
described as Georgian but the lyrics are closer to Blake's *Songs of
Innocence* than to any such attending to natural surfaces. Most
of them aspire to visionary statement—statement, not evocation or description—as in 'To a Child', the first stanza of which
was the one that pleased its author by its 'weightlessness':

> Child do not go
> Into the dark places of the soul,
> For there the grey wolves whine,
> The lean grey wolves.
>
> I have been down
> Among the unholy ones who tear
> Beauty's white robe and clothe her
> In rags of prayer.
>
> Child there is light somewhere
> Under a star,
> Sometime it will be for you
> A window that looks
> Inward to God.

Well, maybe so. But the whole thing's weightless enough to
float past you. The trouble is that romantic clichés like 'dark
places of the soul' and 'Beauty's white robe' may be counters for
genuine insight but we miss the experience even if we get the
meaning. Yet implicit in the 'I' of the poem, in this man who has
come through (whatever), this seer in the pristine sense, is the
'comic' Kavanagh of the later poems. The persona in most of
these apprentice pieces has a notion of 'the main purpose/
Which is to be/Passive, observing with a steady eye'. In the last
stanza of 'To a Blackbird', for example, the wise passiveness of
the Canal Bank sonnets is rehearsed:

> We dream as Earth's sad children
> Go slowly by
> Pleading for our conversion
> With the Most High.

But it is only when this ethereal literary voice incarnates itself in the imagery of the actual world that its messages of transcendence become credible. When the poet stands at the centre of his world, speaking as king or exile, instead of meting and mincing out his voice through the ventriloquist's doll of a mystical exquisite, he does indeed 'find a star-lovely art/In the dark sod.'

Those lines could stand as commentary on the much anthologized lyrics of Kavanagh's early Monaghan period, of which 'Shancoduff', 'A Christmas Childhood', 'Spraying the Potatoes' and the verses 'from *Tarry Flynn*' are the most outstanding. All of these make the home territory 'a theme for kings', 'part of no earthly estate', turn the black hills into 'Alps'. Their kingmaking explorations make possible the regal authority of the later 'Epic' which is their magnificent coda and represents Kavanagh's comprehension of his early achievement. They give body to the assertion in 'Art McCooey' that poetry is shaped 'awkwardly but alive in the unmeasured womb', a womb which is the equivalent of what he called elsewhere 'the unconscious fog'. What we have in these poems are matter-of-fact landscapes, literally presented, but contemplated from such a point of view and with such intensity that they become 'a prospect of the mind'. They are not poems about 'roots'—*The Green Fool* (1938), his first autobiography where he mediates between his audience and his territory with a knowing sociological wink, has more of that kind of self-consciousness—any more than Wordsworth's 'spots of time' in *The Prelude* are about 'roots': their concern is, indeed, the growth of a poet's mind.

It is significant the way the word 'poet' keeps turning up in these poems, used with certainty, to dramatize the speaker in an absolute way. 'A poet' owns the hungry hills of Shancoduff, a 'poet' is lost to potato-fields in the spraying poem, a 'child-poet' picks out letters in 'A Christmas Childhood', and on each occasion the word slews the poem towards a resolution. If we compare such usages, and the 'poet' of 'Inniskeen Road', with earlier *Plowman* lyrics—'O pagan poet you/And I are one' ('To a Blackbird') and 'Her name was poet's grief' ('Mary')—we can see a new authority and boldness. There he was a postulant, full of uninitiated piety towards the office, now he has taken orders, has ordained himself and stands up in Monaghan as the cele-brant of his own mysteries. The word is used as the sign of the imagination, a fiat and an amen. Kavanagh's Monaghan is his pastoral care in the sacerdotal as much as in the literary sense.

Yet his destiny was to become a mendicant rather than a parish priest, called from his 'important places' in Monaghan to consecrate new ground for himself on the banks of the Grand Canal in Dublin, to end up, not like his own 'Father Mat', 'a part of the place,/Natural as a round stone in a grass field', but as an embittered guru. *Tarry Flynn* (1948) is his delightful realization of the call to leave, the pivot and centre of Kavanagh's work, an autobiographical fiction full of affection for and impatience with his parish. This book brings to fruition the valediction to 'every blooming thing' promised in 'Inniskeen Road' and in it Kavanagh achieves his first and fullest articula-tion of his comic vision, that view from Parnassus which was the one sustaining myth or doctrine he forged completely for him-self. Towards the end of the novel there is an account of Tarry retreating to his upstairs room to compose verse, which is at once an account of the novel's genesis and an explication of Kavanagh's subsequent insistence on the poet's detachment, his duty merely 'to state the position':

> This corner was his Parnassus, the constant point above time. Winter and summer since his early boyhood he had sat here and the lumps of candle-grease on the scaly table of the old machine told a story . . .
> The net of earthly intrigue could not catch him here. He was on a level with the horizon—and it was a level on which there was laughter. Looking down at his own misfortunes he thought them funny now. From this height he could even see himself losing his temper with the Finnegans and the Carlins and hating his neigh-bours and he moved the figures on the landscape, made them speak, and was filled with joy in his own power.

Still, despite this celebration of detachment, much of Kavanagh's poetry is born out of a quarrel between 'the grip of the little fields' and 'the City of Kings/Where art, music, letters are the real things'. In *A Soul for Sale* (1947), besides the lyrics of unconscious joy, there are poems of greater emotional complexity, more sombre in tone, more meditative than lyric, the best of which are 'Bluebells for Love' and 'Advent', poems which attempt to renew in the face of experience an insouciance that has been diminished and endangered by too much 'tasting and testing'. And there is a sonnet sequence—how often, by the way, Kavanagh finds the discipline of this form a releasing one—called 'Temptation in Harvest' where the last four sections beautifully and wistfully annotate what the poet was later to describe somewhat melodramatically as 'the worst mistake of my life', his move to Dublin in 1939. This was in retrospect: in the verse, his departure appears as simple obedience to his muse:

> Now I turn
> Away from the ricks, the sheds, the cabbage garden,
> The stones of the street, the thrush song in the tree,
> The potato-pits, the flaggers in the swamp;
> From the country heart that hardly learned to harden,
> From the spotlight of an old-fashioned kitchen lamp
> I go to follow her who winked at me.

Kavanagh's most celebrated poem, however, is about a man who did not follow the hints of his imagination. *The Great Hunger*, first published in 1942 and collected in *A Soul for Sale*, is Kavanagh's rage against the dying of the light, a kind of elegy in a country farmyard, informed not by heraldic notions of seasonal decline and mortal dust but by an intimacy with actual clay and a desperate sense that life in the secluded spot is no book of pastoral hours but an enervating round of labour and lethargy. The poem comes across initially with great documentary force, so that one might be inclined to agree with Kavanagh's characterization of it as being 'concerned with the woes of the poor' as the whole story, but that is only part of the truth, though admittedly the larger part of it.

Nevertheless, the art of the poem is replete with fulfilments and insights for which the protagonist is famished. It is written in a voice urgent and opulent as 'the mill-race heavy with the Lammas floods curving over the weir', (weightiness rather than weightlessness is the virtue here), in a verse that can 'invoke a particular condition of mind' and discovers 'a method of getting at life'. It is the nearest Kavanagh ever gets to a grand style, one that seeks not a continuous decorum but a mixture of modes, of high and low, to accommodate his double perspective, the tragic and the emerging comic. It modulates from open to stanzaic forms, and manages to differentiate nicely between the authentic direct speech of the characters and its own narrative voice which is a selection and heightening of that very speech. Kavanagh's technical achievement here is to find an Irish note that is not dependent on backward looks towards the Irish tradition, not an artful retrieval of poetic strategies from another tongue but a ritualistic drawing out of patterns of run and stress in the English language as it is spoken in Ireland. It is as if the 'stony grey soil of Monaghan' suddenly became vocal. 'Clay is the word and clay is the flesh.'

The poem is the obverse of Kavanagh's *bildungsroman, Tarry Flynn*. It is not about growing up and away but about growing down and in. Its symbol is the potato rather than the potato blossom, its elements are water and earth rather than fire and air, its theme is consciousness moulded in and to the dark rather than opening to the light. It is significant, for example, how Stephen Dedalus's metaphor of nets ('When the soul of a man is born in this country there are nets flung at it to hold it back from flight. You talk to me of nationality, language, religion. I shall try to fly by those nets') is repeated and revised in Kavanagh's presentation of Patrick Maguire:

> The drills slipped by and the days slipped by
> And he trembled his head away and ran free from the world's
> halter,
> And thought himself wiser than any man in the townland
> When he laughed over pints of porter
> Of how he came free from every net spread
> In the gaps of experience. He shook a knowing head ...

The nets that Maguire eludes are those very experiences whose reality Stephen Dedalus goes 'to encounter for the millionth time'. Maguire's running free of the world's halter involves an evasion of those chances 'to err, to fall' which Stephen embraces. His 'knowing head' looks out from under the meshes of family and church ties. Where Stephen disobeyed his mother and defied her pious devotion, fearful of the deleterious 'chemistry' that such obeisance might set up in his soul, Maguire succumbs to 'the lie that is a woman's screen/Around a conscience where soft thighs are spread'. When she told him to 'go to Mass and pray and confess your sins/And you'll have all the luck', 'her son took it as literal truth'. His sexual timidity is continuously related to his failure to achieve any fullness of personality: when he 'makes the field his bride' he settles for 'that metaphysical land/Where flesh was a thought more spiritual than music'.

But not only does the poem refract the Joycean motif, it consciously rejects the Yeatsian 'dream of the noble and the beggarman'. It is a rebuke to the idea of the peasant as noble savage and a dramatization of what its author called 'the usual barbaric life of the Irish country poor'. Against the paternalistic magnificence of

> John Synge, I, and Augusta Gregory thought
> All that we did, all that we said or sang
> Must come from contact with the soil, from that
> Contact everything, Antaeus-like, grew strong

—against this we must set Section XII of the Kavanagh poem which answers it with a vision of 'the peasant ploughman who is half a vegetable', 'a sick horse nosing around the meadow for a clean place to die'.

Yet while these twists help us to see *The Great Hunger*'s place in modern Irish literature, what gives it its essential impetus is not the literary context but its appetite for the living realities of Patrick Maguire's world, and the feeling generated by the disparity between Maguire's and Kavanagh's response to that world. What would be present to Maguire as work and weather, for example, are transformed by the poetry into matters of love and celebration:

> The fields were bleached white,
> The wooden tubs full of water
> Were white in the winds
> That blew through Brannagan's Gap on their way from Siberia;
> The cows on the grassless heights
> Followed the hay that had wings—
> The February fodder that hung itself on the black branches
> Of the hilltop hedge.
> A man stood beside a potato-pit
> And clapped his arms
> And pranced on the crisp roots
> And shouted to warm himself.

In the words of a later poem, 'naming these things is the love-act
and its pledge', and despite the poem's overt anatomy of bar-
renness, there is a conjugal relationship between its language
and its world which conveys a sense of abundance. If Maguire's
satisfaction is to masturbate over the ashes, Kavanagh's is to
allow the imagination to roam studlike in the cold fields. The
poem accumulates a number of incidents in which the
fallow/fertile and the repression/fulfilment contrasts are
dramatized, and simultaneously it establishes the prevailing
atmosphere of futility in which these incidents occur:

> A wonderful night, we had. Duffy's place
> Is very convenient. Is that a ghost or a tree?
> And so they go home with dragging feet
> And their voices rumble like lade carts.
> And they are happy as the dead or sleeping ...
> I should have led that ace of hearts.

If Maguire is blamed, he is also explained—'the poet merely
states the position'—and the position is that Maguire's soul is
never born. The self he achieves is one dressed to fit the
constricting circumstances of home, community and church.
His sexuality is dammed or leaked at the hearth or harnessed to
'probe in the insensitive hair' of the potato crop; his sense of
wonder is calloused by habit so he misses the chance to find
'health and wealth and love' in 'bits and pieces of Everyday'; the
pinnacle of his intellectual ambitions is determined by the
community, to rise to a 'professorship' like

> the pig-gelder Nallon whose knowledge was amazing.
> 'A treble, full multiple odds ... That's flat porter ...
> My turnips are destroyed with the blackguardly crows ...'

and his religious sensibilities atrophy, to be replaced by 'an old
judge's pose:/Respectability and righteousness'.

But there is no condescension in this. It is a loving portrait
which Kavanagh was to reject because 'it lacks the nobility and
repose of poetry'. It is true that there are strident moments,
especially at the end when

> The hungry fiend
> Screams the apocalypse of clay
> In every corner of this land,

125

yet I do not feel that the apostrophizing of the Imagination at the beginning and the end involves a loss of repose. One can see that the poem's fundamentally tragic note is subsumed into the comic vision of *Tarry Flynn* and that it is a step on the way to that vision, yet if *The Great Hunger* did not exist, a greater hunger would, the hunger of a culture for its own image and expression. It is a poem of its own place and time, transposing the griefs of the past—its title conventionally refers to the Great Famine of the 1840s—into the distress of the present, as significant in the Irish context as Hardy's novels were in the English, socially committed but also committed to a larger, more numinous concept of love whose function he decreed was not to look back but 'to look on'.

While the phrase 'socially committed' would have been repellent to Kavanagh, it does remind us that he was a child of the thirties, as depressed and more repressed in Ireland than elsewhere. And while he abjured, in his prose of the 1950s and 1960s, any 'messianic impulse', he was always as concerned in his own way as Yeats was about 'unity of culture' and 'unity of being'. His acute sense of the need to discriminate between 'parochial' and 'provincial' mentalities, his reaction against the romantic nationalist revival of Synge and Yeats as 'a thorough-going English-bred lie', his refusal to allow social and religious differences within the country to be glossed over in a souped-up 'buckleppin' idiom, his almost Arnoldian concern for touchstones of excellence—*Ulysses, Moby Dick*—and his search for an art that would be an Olympian 'criticism of life', all this surfaces in his essays from an overall concern for the 'quality of life' in the country, especially the literary life:

> I am beginning to think there may be such a thing as a Celtic mind which lives on no sustained diet, but on day-to-day journalism. On reflection, I begin to see that this unfaith is not local to Ireland. Yeats, for all his emphasis on Ireland, was the last great Victorian poet. His work was born within the safety of that large, smug, certain world where no one questioned how much was being taken for granted.
> Whatever be the reason, it appears to me that we cannot go on

126

much longer without finding an underlying faith upon which to build our world of letters.

Because of their absence of faith, the anger of men like O'Connor and O'Casey is worthless and even pitiful. ('Poetry and Pietism')

The essays of the 1950s and the 1960s are full of such sweeping remarks. In Dublin he seems to have been pulled in two directions: to be the poet as outsider, as parishioner of Monaghan— and the criticism in *Kavanagh's Weekly* (1952) as well as the satire in *Come Dance with Kitty Stobling* (1960) is generated by this desire to be on the one hand the parochial precursor in provincial Dublin; yet on the other hand, there is an implicit wish to be a parishioner of Ireland, to be the poet as integral part of a whole parochial culture. Much of what he says is a plea for an ideal national culture but it is premised on the rejection of nationality as a category in cultural life. In Dublin his Monaghan sceptre becomes a forked stick, that only occasionally works as a divining rod, as on the banks of the Grand Canal or in the environs of 'The Hospital'. In the end he finds himself at bay in that new parish which he called his 'Pembrokeshire', a domain that was again 'part of no earthly estate', centring on Baggot Street Bridge. Over and over again he reverts to his experience of a poetic rebirth in these surroundings:

I have been thinking of making my grove on the banks of the Grand Canal near Baggot Street Bridge where in recent days I redis-covered my roots. My hegira was to the Grand Canal bank where again I saw the beauty of water and green grass and the magic of light. It was the same emotion I had known when I stood on a sharp slope in Monaghan ...

It should be said that this shift or tremor that released his new sense of his powers was occasioned by considerable emotional and physical distress. In 1952 he had been the victim of a notorious profile in a magazine called *The Leader* and had later conducted an unsuccessful libel action against the magazine, during which his cross-questioning in the witness-box became something of a spectator sport for Dubliners. That was in 1954 and shortly afterwards he underwent an operation for lung cancer. So the Parnassian calm which he conjures in these first redemptive sonnets represents both aesthetic and spiritual resourcefulness:

I learned, I learned—when one might be inclined
To think, too late, you cannot recover your losses—
I learned something of the nature of God's mind,
Not the abstract Creator but He who caresses
The daily and nightly earth; He who refuses
To take failure for an answer till again and again is worn.

('Miss Universe')

Still, despite the generous epiphanies represented by the best work of his last decade, Kavanagh's face inclines to set like Maguire's in a judicial pose. Despite the accuracy and serious implications of his critical *aperçus*, despite the continuous vaunting of the comic point of view, the overall impression to be got from reading the second half of the *Collected Poems* is of a man who knows he can do the real thing but much of the time straining and failing. He should not simply be taken at his own word on the superiority of his comic vision, the supremacy of 'not caring' as a philosophy of life. When it serves as a myth for entrancement, for Franciscan acceptance, and approaches the condition of charity, as it does in the Canal Bank sonnets and in meditations like 'Intimate Parnassus'; or when it is guaranteed by the purgatorial experiences on which it is based as in 'The Hospital', 'Miss Universe', 'Prelude', 'Auditors in', 'If Ever You Go to Dublin Town' and in a song like 'On Raglan Road'; or when it is offered as a poetic with the rhythmic heave of 'Yellow Vestment'—then Kavanagh is 'embodying' rather than 'knowing' the truth of it, and the old sense of a man at once marooned and in possession, impatient and in love, pervades the verse, and the verse itself is supplied with energy from below and beyond its occasion.

But too often the doctrine that 'poetry is a mystical thing and a dangerous thing' was used as a petrified stick to beat the world with. Too much of the satire in *Come Dance with Kitty Stobling* remains doggerel ensnared in the environment which it purports to disdain. The pleasures to be derived from 'Adventures in the Bohemian Jungle' or 'The Christmas Mummers' are those of a ringside seat at a cockpit where the fight is lively but untidy and ends without a kill. And as for squibs like 'Irish

Stew', 'Spring Day', 'Who Killed James Joyce?' and 'Portrait of the Artist', they simply represent an inelegant opportunism:

> Did you get money
> For your Joycean knowledge?
> I got a scholarship
> To Trinity College.
>
> I made the pilgrimage
> In the Bloomsday swelter
> From the Martello Tower
> To the cabby's shelter.
>
> ('Who Killed James Joyce?')

If my memory is right, one of the best-known photographs of Kavanagh is with Brian O'Nolan on a Bloomsday outing.

Paradoxically, such poems contribute to an idea of the poet that Kavanagh was at pains to disassociate himself from in his essay on 'The Irish Tradition': 'One of the Irish ideas of the poet is of the uproarious clown. I have hardly ever heard an Irish admirer of Gaelic or any other poetry speaking of the poet that he didn't give the impression that he thought it all a great joke.' Unfortunately, Kavanagh's spirited living out of his idea of the autocracy of the personality often furnished fuel for such an attitude, and a performance like 'Sensational Disclosures! (Kavanagh Tells All)' treads a very dangerous line between exploiting and excoriating it. When he formulated the mood of such regenerative poems as 'Canal Bank Walk' into the desire 'to play a true note on a dead slack string' he too often ended up, as the *Collected Poems* end up, 'In Blinking Blankness', making an aesthetic out of self-pity, formally cornered, so that doggerel seemed the only appropriate mode for an exploration of the self, a form not very conducive to 'nobility and repose'.

Kavanagh's achievement lies in the valency of a body of individual poems which establish the purity, authority and authenticity of his voice rather than in any plotted cumulative force of the opus as a whole. It could be said of him (as Thomas Kinsella has said of Austin Clarke) that his *Selected Poems* would be the marvellous book, more cogent and coherent than the *Collected*. If I feel that the man who suffered was not fully recompensed by the man who created, Kavanagh felt it too. Without myth, without masters, 'No System, no Plan', he lived

129

from hand to mouth and unceremoniously where Yeats—and Sidney—fed deliberately and ritually, in the heart's rag-and-bone shop. And one might say that when he had consumed the roughage of his Monaghan experience, he ate his heart out.

Reprinted from *Two Decades of Irish Writing,*
ed. Douglas Dunn, Carcanet Press, 1975

The Sense of Place

I think there are two ways in which place is known and cherished, two ways which may be complementary but which are just as likely to be antipathetic. One is lived, illiterate and unconscious, the other learned, literate and conscious. In the literary sensibility, both are likely to co-exist in a conscious and unconscious tension: this tension and the poetry it produces are what I want to discuss. I want to consider how the different senses of Ireland, of Northern Ireland, and of specific places on our island, have affected poets over these last hundred years.

I might have begun the exploration much further back, of course, because in Irish poetry there is a whole genre of writing called *dinnseanchas*, poems and tales which relate the original meanings of place names and constitute a form of mythological etymology. An early epic like the *Tain bo Cuailgne* is full of incidental *dinnseanchas*, insofar as it connects various incidents on the journey of the Connacht armies from Cruachan to Carlingford with the names of places as we now know them, or at least as they were known in the Gaelic past. Ardee, for example, the town in Co. Louth. In Irish, Ardee means Ferdia's Ford, and it was at this point (at a ford on the River Fane) that Cuchullain and Ferdia, brothers in arms in their youth, fought their great single combat by day and tended each other's wounds by night until Cuchullain slew Ferdia with his magical weapon, the *gae bolga*. It is a story that would have been current in everybody's mind when Irish was the *lingua franca* and it is still one of the best known and best loved legends in the Ulster cycle. So the place name, Ardee, succinctly marries the legendary and the local.

It now requires some small degree of learning to know this

131

about Ardee. We have to retrieve the underlay of Gaelic legend in order to read the full meaning of the name and to flesh out the topographical record with its human accretions. The whole of the Irish landscape, in John Montague's words, is a manuscript which we have lost the skill to read. When we go as tourists to Donegal or Connemara or Kerry we go with at best an aesthetic eye, comforting ourselves with the picturesqueness of it all or rejoicing in the fact that it is unspoiled. We will have little felt knowledge of the place, little enough of a sense of wonder or a sense of tradition. Tory Island, Knocknarea, Slieve Patrick, all of them deeply steeped in associations from the older culture, will not stir us beyond a visual pleasure unless that culture means something to us, unless the features of the landscape are a mode of communion with a something other than themselves, a something to which we ourselves still feel we might belong.

On the other hand, as we pass south along the coast from Tory to Knocknarea, we go through the village of Drumcliff and under Ben Bulben, we skirt Lissadell and Innisfree. All of these places now live in the imagination, all of them stir us to responses other than the merely visual, all of them are instinct with the spirit of a poet and his poetry. Irrespective of our creed or politics, irrespective of what culture or subculture may have coloured our individual sensibilities, our imaginations assent to the stimulus of the names, our sense of the place is enhanced, our sense of ourselves as inhabitants not just of a geographical country but of a country of the mind is cemented. It is this feeling, assenting, equable marriage between the geographical country and the country of the mind, whether that country of the mind takes its tone unconsciously from a shared oral inherited culture, or from a consciously savoured literary culture, or from both, it is this marriage that constitutes the sense of place in its richest possible manifestation.

That metaphor of marriage can lead us a bit further in our exploration, insofar as marriage is something that for centuries survived in the realms of the sacred, but now is thought about and sometimes survives in the realm of the secular. Similarly with our sense, or—better still—our *sensing* of place. It was once more or less sacred. The landscape was sacramental, instinct with signs, implying a system of reality beyond the visible realities. Only thirty years ago, and thirty miles from Belfast, I

132

think I experienced this kind of world vestigially and as a result
may have retained some vestigial sense of place as it was experienced in the older dispensation. As I walked to school, I saw
Lough Beg from Mulholland's Brae, and the spire of Church
Island rose out of the trees. On Church Island Sunday in
September, there was a pilgrimage out to the island, because St.
Patrick was supposed to have prayed there, and prayed with
such intensity that he branded the shape of his knee into a stone
in the old churchyard. The rainwater that collected in that
stone, of course, had healing powers, and the thorn bush beside
it was pennanted with the rags used by those who rubbed their
warts and sores in that water. Then on a clear day, out in the
Antrim hills beyond Lough Beg, I could see the unmistakable
hump of Slemish, the mountain where the youthful Patrick had
tended sheep. That legend, and the ringing ascetic triumph of
the lines in his *Confession* where he talks about rising in the frosts
of winter to pray to his Christian God, all combined to give
Slemish a nimbus of its own, and made it more potent in the
mind's eye than Slieve Gallon, a bigger, closer mountain that
we faced on the road home from school, and which took its aura
from our song '*Slieve Gallon's Braes*'. On Aughrim Hill,
between the school and the lough, somebody had found an old
sword, deemed to be a Viking sword, since we knew those
almost legendary people had sailed the Bann a thousand years
before; and on a shelf in the master's room there was a bit of
wood that had been turned to stone by the action of the waters of
Lough Neagh.

There, if you like, was the foundation for a marvellous or a
magical view of the world, a foundation that sustained a
diminished structure of lore and superstition and half-pagan,
half-Christian thought and practice. Much of the flora of the
place had a religious force, especially if we think of the root of
the word in *religare*, to bind fast. The single thorn-tree bound
us to a notion of the potent world of fairies, and when my father
cut such a thorn, retribution was seen to follow inexorably when
the horse bolted in harness, broke its leg and had to be
destroyed. The green rushes bound us to the beneficent spirit of
St. Brigid: cut on Brigid's Eve, the first of February, they were
worked into Brigid's crosses that would deck the rooms and
outhouses for the rest of the year. Indeed, one of my most

133

cherished and in some way mysterious memories is of an old neighbour of ours called Annie Devlin sitting in the middle of a floor strewn with green rushes, a kind of local sybil, plaiting the rushes and plaiting all of us into that ritualized way of life.

Then on May Eve, the buttercups and ladysmock appeared on the windowsills in obedience to some rite, and during the month of May the pagan goddess became the Virgin Mary and May flowers had to be gathered for her altar on the chest-of-drawers in the bedroom, so that the primroses and the celandines also wound us into the sacral and were wound into it in their turn. Late summer, and my father plaited harvest bows from the new corn and wore them in his lapel. Hallowe'en, and the turnip, that homely and densely factual root, became a root of some kind of evil as the candle blazed in it from a gatepost in the dark. At the fireside then, the talk of old times when cows were blinked and men met the devil in the shape of a goat or heard him as a tinkle of chains on the road after dark, or saw him, or powers of some sort, in lights dancing in spots where no lights should be. Such naming of examples is a pleasure to me, and that is, I believe, itself an earnest of the power of place.

But of course it wasn't just the old religion that exhaled its fragrances in that place. The more recent sectarian varieties were also intimately bound up with different locales. The red, white and blue flagpost at the Hillhead, for example, was a totem that possessed all the force of a holy mountain, and the green chestnut tree that flourished at the entrance to the Gaelic Athletic Association grounds was more abundantly green from being the eminence where the tricolour was flown illicitly at Easter or on sports days. Even Annie Devlin's rich and overgrown garden, with its shooting leeks and roofings of rhubarb leaves, even that natural earth was tinctured with the worst aspects of our faiths, insofar as that lovely flower, Sweet William, became suspect in the imagination from its connection with William of Orange, the king we sent to hell regularly up the long ladder and down the short rope.

All this was actual, all of it was part of the ordinary round if only a part of it, but all of it has by now a familiar literary ring to it. And if it has, that is partly due to a new found pride in our own places that flourished suddenly in the late nineteenth century and resulted in a new literature, a revived interest in

134

folklore, a movement to revive the Irish language, and in general a determination to found or re-found a native tradition. At a time when the spirit of the age was becoming increasingly scientific and secular, when Sir James Frazer's *Golden Bough* was seeking to banish the mystery from the old faiths and standardize and anatomize the old places, Yeats and his friends embarked upon a deliberately counter-cultural movement to reinstate the fairies, to make the world more magical than materialistic, and to elude the social and political interpretations of society in favour of a legendary and literary vision of race.

Although it has long been fashionable to smile indulgently at the Celtic Twilight, it has to be remembered that the movement was the beginning of a discovery of confidence in our own ground, in our place, in our speech, English and Irish. And it seems to me undeniable that Yeats's sense of the otherness of his Sligo places led him to seek for a language and an imagery other than the ones which were available to him in the aesthetic modes of literary London.

He had, of course, a double purpose. One, to restore a body of old legends and folk beliefs that would bind the people of the Irish place to the body of their world, in much the way that I have suggested the name Ardee meshes the old saga with the Ardee man's sense of who he is and where he is. Yeats in this way would have commended the remark made by Carson McCullers, that to know who you are, you have to have a place to come from. But his other purpose was to supplement this restored sense of historical place with a new set of associations that would accrue when a modern Irish literature, rooted in its own region and using its own speech, would enter the imaginations of his countrymen. And the classic moment in this endeavour was his meeting with Synge, in a hotel in Paris, the young Synge in search of *la vie de bohème*, struggling with the idioms of decadence, whom Yeats sent west to express the life of Aran, in the language of the tribe. At that moment a new country of the mind was conceived in English, the west that the poets imagined, full of tragic fishermen and poetic peasants.

Synge, in his preface to *The Tinker's Wedding*, used a phrase which is apposite to my concerns in this discussion. 'The drama is made serious,' he wrote, 'not by the degree in which it is taken up with problems that are serious in themselves, but by the degree in which it gives the nourishment, not very easy to define, on which our imaginations live.' That nourishment, it seems to me, became available more abundantly to us as a result of the achievements of the Irish Literary Revival, and much of its imaginative protein was extracted from the sense of place. There is, for example, this short but very revealing moment in a review which Yeats wrote in 1874, when he was twenty-nine. 'The final test of the value of any work of art to our particular needs, is when we place it in the hierarchy of those recollections which are our standards and our beacons. At the head of mine are a certain night scene long ago, when I heard the wind blowing in a bed of reeds by the border of a little lake, a Japanese picture of cranes flying through a blue sky, and a line or two out of Homer.' Yeats is here talking about what Matthew Arnold called 'touchstones', high points of imaginative experience, 'those recollections which are our standards and our beacons'. Arnold's touchstones were literary, drawn from the whole field of European poetry, but it is typical and significant, I think, that first in the hierarchy of Yeats's recollections is an experience that was obviously local and deeply involved with his apprehension of the spirit of a place. The wind among those night reeds stayed with him and was so pervasive in his mental weather that it formed the title of a collection of poems that he published four years later, a book that brought the moods of the Irish weather into English poetry and changed the atmosphere of that poetry.

However, we have to understand also that this nourishment which springs from knowing and belonging to a certain place and a certain mode of life is not just an Irish obsession, nor is the relationship between a literature and a locale with its common language a particularly Irish phenomenon. It is true, indeed, that we have talked much more about it in this country because of the peculiar fractures in our history, north and south, and because of the way that possession of the land and possession of different languages have rendered the question particularly urgent. But I like to remember that Dante was very much a man of a particular place, that his great poem is full of intimate placings and place-names, and that as he moves round the murky circles of hell, often heard rather than seen by his damned friends and enemies, he is recognized by his local speech or so recognizes them. And we could also talk about the sense of place in English poetry and find it rewarding with talents as diverse as Tennyson and Auden, Arnold and John Clare, Edward Thomas and Geoffrey Hill.

But I want to turn the plough back into the home ground again and see what can be turned up in Co. Monaghan. Patrick Kavanagh's place was to a large extent his subject. As I have said before (see p. 121) his quarrel with himself was the quarrel between himself and it, between the illiterate self that was tied to the little hills and earthed in the stony grey soil, and the literate self that pined for 'the city of Kings/Where art, music and letters were the real things'. His sonnet 'Epic' is his comprehension of this about himself and his affirmation of the profound importance of the parochial. Where Yeats had a conscious cultural and, in the largest sense, political purpose in his hallowing of Irish regions, Kavanagh had no such intent. Yeats would have probably called him local rather that national, as he had called William Allingham; and Kavanagh would have called himself parochial. He abjured any national purpose, any belief in Ireland as 'a spiritual entity'. And yet, ironically, Kavanagh's work probably touches the majority of Irish people more immediately and more intimately than most things in Yeats. I am not going to say that this makes Kavanagh a more important writer, but what I do say is that Kavanagh's fidelity to the unpromising, unspectacular countryside of Monaghan and his rendering of the authentic speech of those parts gave the majority of Irish people, for whom the experience of life on the land was perhaps the most formative, an image of themselves that nourished their sense of themselves in that serious way which Synge talked about in his preface. Kavanagh's grip on our imaginations stems from our having attended the intimate hedge-school that he attended. For thirty years and more he lived the life of a small farmer's son in the parish of Inniskeen, the life of fairs and football matches, of mass-going and dance-going. He shared his neighbours' fundamental piety, their flyness, their brusque manners and their vigorous speech. He gambled and rambled among them. He bought and sold land and cattle and corn. Yet all the time, as he stitched himself into the outer patterns of his place, there was a sensitivity and a yearning that distinguished him. For this poet whom we recognize as being the voice of a communal life had a fiercely individual sense of himself. 'A poet is never one of the people', he declared in his *Self Portrait*. 'He is detached, remote, and the life of small-time dances and talk about football would not be for him. He might take part but he could not belong.' And that statement could stand as a gloss on the first important poem that Kavanagh wrote, a poem which is about his distance from what is closest to him, a poem too where the life of small-time dances which he affects to disdain is lovingly particularized (see p. 117).

I said there that 'Inniskeen Road, July Evening' is a love poem to a place and I noted the way that that adjective 'blooming' pulls in two directions at once, faithful to the local and dialect meaning in 'blooming' as a word expressing impatience, and faithful also to the literary charge in it as a word that celebrates growth and flourish. And the same vigour comes out in another little word that is like a capillary root leading down into the whole sensibility of Kavanagh's place. In the first line, 'the bicycles go by in twos and threes'. They do not 'pass by' or 'go past', as they would in a more standard English voice or place, and in that little touch Kavanagh touches what I am circling. He is letting the very life blood of the place in that one minute incision. The words 'go by' and 'blooming', moreover, are natural and spoken; they are not used as a deliberate mark of folksiness or as a separate language, in the way that Irish speech is ritualized by Synge. Inniskeen English is not used as a picturesque idiom but as the writer's own natural speech and again this points to Kavanagh's essential difference from the Revival writers. There is nothing programmed about his diction, or about his world. 'Who owns them hungry hills?' says the ungrammatical cattle-jobber in the poem 'Shancoduff' but as he speaks we know that the poet is neither savouring nor disdaining 'them hills' as opposed to 'those hills'. The poet meets his people at eye-level, he hears them shouting through the hedge and not through the chinks in a loft floor, the way Synge heard his literary speech in Co. Wicklow.

'I heard the Duffy's shouting "Damn your soul"', Kavanagh tells us in 'Epic' and the very ordinariness of the quarrel

between the Duffys and McCabes makes him again impatient of
the whole blooming crowd of them:

> That was the year of the Munich bother. Which
> Was more important? I inclined
> To lose my faith in Ballyrush and Gortin
> Till Homer's ghost came whispering to my mind.
> He said: I made the Iliad from such
> A local row. Gods make their own importance.

In this case, the local idiom extends beyond the locale itself.
Munich, the European theatre, is translated into the local
speech to become bother, and at once it is bother, it has become
knowable, and no more splendid than the bother at home.
Language, as well as gods, makes its own importance: the sense
of place issues in a point of view, a phrase that Kavanagh set
great store by and used always as a positive. He cherished the
ordinary, the actual, the known, the unimportant.

> Parochialism is universal; it deals with the fundamentals. It is not
> by the so-called national dailies that people who emigrate keep in
> touch with their roots. In London, outside the Catholic churches,
> the big run is on the local Irish papers. Lonely on Highgate Hill
> outside St. Joseph's Church I rushed to buy my *Dundalk Democrat*
> and reading it I was back in my native fields. Now that I analyse
> myself I realize that throughout everything I write, there is this
> constantly recurring motif of the need to go back. . . . So it is for
> these reasons that I return to the local newspapers. Who has died?
> Who has sold his farm?

Perhaps I can clarify something more of Kavanagh's relation to
his place if I compare that relationship with another poet's
relationship to his region. North of Monaghan lies Tyrone, and
it is very much as a Tyrone poet that John Montague locates
himself in a large section of his work. In an essay contributed to
the *Irish Times* some years ago, Montague wrote about his
relation to his place and also ended up with a feminine image of
it, but it is a very different image from Kavanagh's. Since the
piece bears so closely to the whole of what I have been saying so
far about the sense of place, I want to quote from it at some
length:

> A month ago, I was lying on the side of a hill, looking at one of the
> loveliest landscapes in Ireland. I was just back from a short reading

tour in America, where I had earned more in a month than a term's teaching at home would bring. But at no point in my journey, even crossing a sunlit campus after my morning's stint was done, or relaxing in some heated pool, was I as happy as that May day, on the slopes of Sliabh Gullion.

Everything seemed to share that prehistoric timelessness; the stream that ran down the edge of the mountain path, the sheep that scattered as one climbed to the dark glitter of the Hag's Lake . . .

Take the name Knockmany. One could explain it as 'Cnoc Maine', the hill of the Manaig or Menapii, a tribe of the Belgae who travelled as far as Lough Erne; after all, they gave their name to the adjoining county of Fermanagh. But the local translation of the name is Ania's Cove, and Ania or Aine or Ano is the Danaan Mother goddess, whose name is also found in the River Boyne, the Boan or Good Mother. Even Pope pays oblique reverence to her:

> 'And thou, great Anna . . .'

I am beginning to sound like Robert Graves's *White Goddess*, but there is an extraordinary identity between the linguistic and archaeological evidence concerning Knockmany. The curious cup marks and circles have been described as the eyes and breasts of a mother goddess, whose cult spread from Syria. I doubt if the late O. G. S. Crawford knew early Irish, but his eye goddess theory bears out the derivations I have suggested, since the same shapes are found at Newgrange, on the Boyne. So the least Irish place name can net a world with its associations.

Now it is obvious that although both Montague and Kavanagh look and listen with intensity inside their parishes, their eyes and ears seek and pick up different things. Kavanagh's eye has been used to bending over the ground before it ever bent over a book but we feel with Montague that the case is vice versa. If Montague, for example, had been born in Kavanagh's country, Ardee and the Black Pig's Dyke would have figured significantly in his literary topography. But Kavanagh never mentions them. Kavanagh's place names are there to stake out a personal landscape, they declare one man's experience, they are denuded of tribal or etymological implications. Mucker, Dundalk, Inniskeen, provide no *frisson* beyond the starkness of their own dunting, consonantal noises. They are names for what is known and loved, and inhabit the universe of the actual with other words like 'butter', 'collar and reins', 'bull-wire' and 'winkers' as we hear in that risky but successful poem called 'Kerr's Ass':

> We borrowed the loan cf Kerr's big ass
> To go to Dundalk with butter,
> Brought him home the evening before the market
> An exile that night in Mucker.
>
> We heeled up the cart before the door,
> We took the harness inside—
> The straw-stuffed straddle, the broken breeching
> With bits of bull-wire tied;
>
> The winkers that had no choke-bank,
> The collar and the reins...
> In Ealing Broadway, London Town
> I name their several names
>
> Until a world comes to life—
> Morning, the silent bog,
> And the God of imagination waking
> In a Mucker fog.

Kavanagh's place names are used here as posts to fence out a personal landscape. But Montague's are rather sounding lines, rods to plumb the depths of a shared and diminished culture. They are redolent not just of his personal life but of the history of his people, disinherited and dispossessed. What are most resonant and most cherished in the names of Montague's places are their tribal etymological implications.

Both Kavanagh and Montague explore a hidden Ulster, to alter Daniel Corkery's suggestive phrase, and Montague's exploration follows Corkery's tracks in a way that Kavanagh's does not. There is an element of cultural and political resistance and retrieval in Montague's work that is absent from Kavanagh's. What is hidden at the bottom of Montague's region is first of all a pagan civilization centred on the dolmen; then a Gaelic civilization centred on the O'Neill inauguration stone at Tullyhogue. The ancient feminine religion of Northern Europe is the lens through which he looks and the landscape becomes a memory, a piety, a loved mother. The present is suffused with the past. When he walks the mountains and farms of his neighbours, he can think of himself as a survivor, a repository, a bearer and keeper of what had almost been lost. On the other hand, when Kavanagh walks through others' farms, he will think of himself as a trespasser rather than a survivor. His sensibility is acutely of its own time and place, and his region is as deep not as its history but as his own life in it. At the bottom of Kavanagh's imagination there is no pagan queen, no mystique of the national, the mythic or the tribal: instead, there is the childhood piety of the Morning Offering prayer, a prayer which offers to Jesus 'through the most pure hands of Mary all the prayers, works and sufferings of this day for all the intentions of Thy Divine Heart'. I believe that the spirit of this prayer, the child's open-eyed attention to the small and the familiar, is fundamental to Kavanagh's vision, as is the child's religious belief that if each action, however small, is offered up for love, then in the eyes of God it is as momentous in its negligible, casual silence as the great noisy cataclysmic and famous acts that make up history. Compare these two poems and all that I have said becomes, I am sure, simpler and clearer. First, Kavanagh's 'On Reading a Book of Common Wild Flowers':

> O the greater fleabane that grew at the back of the potato pit:
> I often trampled through it looking for rabbit burrows!
> The burnet saxifrage was there in profusion
> And the autumn gentian—
> I knew them all by eyesight long before I knew their names.
> We were in love before we were introduced.
>
> Let me not moralize or have remorse, for these names
> Purify a corner of my mind;
> I jump over them and rub them with my hands,
> And a free moment appears brand new and spacious
> Where I may live beyond the reach of desire.

Here, the book learning disappears and the mind is purified by naming the actual. The imagination slips free of the reading and refreshes itself in the common and humble sights Kavanagh has known in common places. But in this poem by John Montague which also celebrates the flora of his fields, the common and humble vegetation of the hedgerows and headlands assumes all kinds of learning into it. The poem does not elude the learned intelligence but calls upon it. There is first of all the echo of the

Marian litany and through that an appeal to the whole gorgeous liturgy of the Catholic Church; then behind that there is, I feel, an appeal to our sense of early Irish nature poetry, that glorified fern and branch and waterfall; and behind that again there is the notion that the curve of the hill is the curve of a loved one's beauty, its contour the contour of a woman with child.

> Hinge of silence
>> creak for us
> Rose of darkness
>> unfold for us
> Wood anemone
>> sway for us
> Blue harebell
>> bend for us
> Moist fern
>> unfurl for us
> Springy moss
>> uphold us
> Branch of pleasure
>> lean on us
> Leaves of delight
>> murmur for us
> Odorous wood
>> breathe on us
> Evening dews
>> pearl for us
> Freshet of ease
>> flow for us
> Secret waterfall
>> pour for us
> Hidden cleft
>> speak to us
> Portal of delight
>> inflame us
> Hill of motherhood
>> wait for us
> Gate of Birth
>> open for us

Kavanagh's sense of his place involves detachment, Montague's attachment. When Montague asks who he is, he is forced to seek a connection with a history and a heritage; before he affirms a personal identity, he posits a national identity, and his region and his community provide a lifeline to it. Whereas Kavanagh flees the abstractions of nationalism, political or cultural. To find himself, he detaches rather than attaches himself to the communal. *I* rather than *we* is his preferred first person. 'A poet is never one of the people. The life of small-time dances would not be for him . . .' It is just possible that John Montague, if he heard a fiddle played at one of those small-time dances, would be inclined to see in them the last twitch of his ideal culture, and thus envisage such a life as an enabling rather than a disabling phenomenon for the poet.

But however different the focus of Kavanagh and Montague, what they have in common is a feeling for their place that steadies them and gives them a point of view. And just how vital this matter of feeling is we will see if we listen to an account of the Tyrone countryside by Robert Lloyd Praeger in his book, *The Way that I Went*. His sense of the place is, on the whole, that it is no place:

> Now that I wish to write about it, I find it is a curiously negative tract, with a paucity of outstanding features when its size and variety of surface are considered, for it stretches from Lough Neagh to within ten miles of the western sea at Donegal Bay. On its north-eastern frontier stand the Sperrin Mountains, raising broad peat-covered domes of schist and quartzite to over 2000 feet (Sawell, 2240 feet). These hills have been referred to already (p68): they are among the least inspiring of Irish mountains, though on the Derry side some fine glens are found. The only lake to be mentioned in connection with Tyrone is Lough Neagh, also dealt with previously (p95): for fifteen miles it forms the eastern boundary. Here the broad flat shore characteristic of this great lake prevails, and there are bays, and low dunes of sharp silicious sand, much prized for building in Belfast. A minor excitement is provided by the occurrence in this neighbourhood of a small coal-field; the coal is of good quality, but the strata have been so much disturbed by earth-movements that the seams are broken up by faulting, tending to make mining difficult and expensive.

This is also a subjective reaction, of course: who is to say objectively that Tyrone is a 'curiously negative tract' and that the Sperrins are 'the least inspiring of the Irish mountains'? Who (except someone with an incurable taste for punning) will agree that a small coal-field constitutes 'a minor excitement'? The clue to Praeger's sense of place comes a couple of paragraphs later when he moves into Fermanagh and declares it 'more picturesque and from many points of view more interesting'. His point of view is visual, geological, not like Kavanagh's, emotional and definitive. The Tyrone landscape, for him, is not hallowed by associations that come from growing up and thinking oneself in and back into the place. His eye is regulated by laws of aesthetics, by the disciplines of physical geography, and not, to borrow a phrase from Wordsworth, by the primary laws of our nature, the laws of feeling. In fact, Wordsworth was perhaps the first man to articulate the nurture that becomes available to the feelings through dwelling in one dear perpetual place. In his narrative poem, 'Michael', he talks at one point about the way the Westmorland mountains were so much more than a picturesque backdrop for his shepherd's existence, how they were rather companionable and influential in the strict sense of the word 'influential'—things flowed in from them to Michael's psychic life. This Lake District was not inanimate stone but active nature, humanized and humanizing:

And grossly that man errs, who should suppose
That the green valleys, and the streams and rocks,
Were things indifferent to the Shepherd's thoughts.
Fields, where with cheerful spirits he had breathed
The common air; hills, which with vigorous step
He had so often climbed; which had impressed
So many incidents upon his mind
Of hardship, skill or courage, joy or fear;
Which, like a book, preserved the memory
Of the dumb animals, whom he had saved,
Had fed or sheltered, linking to such acts
The certainty of honourable gain;
Those fields, those hills—what could they less—had laid
Strong hold on his affections, were to him
A pleasurable feeling of blind love,
The pleasure which there is in life itself.

And that temperate understanding of the relationship between a person and his place, of the way the surface of the earth can be accepted into and be a steadying influence upon the quiet depths of the mind, leads me to another poet of our places. John

145

Hewitt's poems take their inspiration now from the literate historical reading of his place and its culture, now from the illiterate messages beat out in his pulses as he walks our countryside. He looks at the world now with the analytical and profane eye of a man of the left, now with the affectionate and feeling eye of 'an Ulsterman of Planter stock'. In an entirely pertinent passage of his long poem 'Conacre', written in 1943, he questions himself about his need to repose in the customary and ancestral world of the countryside, in spite of his urban childhood and his politicized intelligence:

> Why not then seize the virtue in my luck,
> and make my theme the riveters who struck
> the other day for solidarity,
> or take a derrick simply as a tree
> and praise a puddle that contains the sky
> for the boots and wheels that clatter by?

He then goes on to accumulate a catalogue of images of city life, images that domesticate him to his native streets, and declares

> These by sound and sight
> Make up the world my heel and nostril know,
> but not the world my pulses take for true.

> ... somehow these close images engage
> the prompt responses only, pity, humour, rage,
> and leave the quiet depths unmeasured still;
> whereas the heathered shoulder of a hill,
> a quick cloud on the meadow, wind-lashed corn,
> black wrinkled haws, grey tufted wool on thorn,
> the high lark singing, the retreating sea—
> these stab the heart with sharp humility
> and prick like water on the thirsty wrist
> in hill spring thrust, when hot sun splits the mist
> among dark peatstacks on long boggy plains,
> such as lie high and black between the Glens,
> or on the crown of Garron struck by sun
> to emerald or rain wrapped. I have won,
> by grace or by intention, to delight
> that seems to match the colours mystics write
> only in places far from kerb or street.

Yet as well as granting that these stirrings of the depths may be 'graces' inhabiting the same element as mystical apprehensions,

146

Hewitt is also in possession of another vocabulary and another mode of understanding. His attachment to his actual countryside involves an attachment to an idea of country: his cherishing of the habitat is symptomatic of his history, and that history is the history of the colonist, who, much like Wordsworth's Michael, has grown to be native to his fields through the accretions of human memory and human associations. There is a pride of assertion at the end of his dramatic monologue, 'The Colony', that does not give the lie to John Montague's proclamation and reclamation of the Ulster territory as Gaelic; but it does give the obstinate colonist's answer:

> We have rights drawn from the soil and sky;
> the use, the pace, the patient years of labour,
> the rain against the lips, the changing light,
> the heavy clay-sucked stride, have altered us;
> we would be strangers in the Capitol;
> this is our country also, no-where else;
> and we shall not be outcast on the world.

It has been said that John Hewitt expresses the crisis of identity experienced by the Planter stock but the identity spoken for and through in these lines seems to me more composed than critical. In the Glens of Antrim this poet senses himself, as his fictional colonist also does, as co-inhabitant but not as kin with the natives. He loves their sacral understanding of their place but cannot share fully what he calls 'the enchantments of the old tree magic'. Hewitt is bound to his region not through the figure of a mythological queen in her aspect as spirit of the place but through the charter given by an historical king. His vision is bifocal, not, as in Montague's case, monocular. When Montague's vision founds itself on the archaeological, it is on Knockmany Dolmen, on the insular tradition. When Hewitt searches for his primeval symbol, it is also megalithic; 'a broken circle of stones on a rough hillside, somewhere,' is the destination of his search for a 'somewhere', and his note tells us that that somewhere is a refraction of two places. '"Circle of stones": for me the archetype of this is the Rollright Stones on the border of Oxfordshire, mingled with the recollection of "Ossian's Grave", Glenaan, Co. Antrim.' Oxfordshire and Antrim, two fidelities, two spirits that, in John Donne's original and active verb, interinanimate each other. John Hewitt knows

147

where he stands and he can also watch himself taking his stand. His civilized mind takes its temper from a political, literary and religious tradition that is English, but his instincts, his eye and ear, are tutored by the Ulster landscape, and it is in the rag-and-bone shop of the instincts that a poetry begins and ends, though it can raise itself by the ladders of intelligence towards a platform and a politics.

It could be said of the poets I have considered that their sense of place is a physical one but I want to turn finally and briefly to three younger writers for whom the sense of place might be termed metaphysical. In the work of Derek Mahon, Michael Longley and Paul Muldoon place symbolizes a personal drama before it epitomizes a communal situation. Mahon's bleak Glengormley and bleaker still North Antrim, Longley's botanically abundant west of Ireland and his nostalgically apprehended bleaching greens, Muldoon's rivery and apple-dappled Armagh, are all places that do not have to be proved or vindicated in the way Kavanagh's Monaghan or Montague's Tyrone or John Hewitt's braes and glens have to be. They exist to serve the poet and not vice versa. None of these poets surrenders himself to the mythology of his place but instead each subdues the place to become an element in his own private mythology. They may be preyed upon in life by the consequences of living on this island now, but their art is a mode of play to outface the predatory circumstances. Muldoon's wry and lyrical wit, Longley's amorous vocabularies, Mahon's visionary desolation are personal poetic gifts, but as the young Yeats once 'sought to weave an always personal emotion into a general pattern of myth and symbol' so these poets weave their individual feelings round places they and we know, in a speech that they and we share; and in a world where the sacral vision of place is almost completely eradicated they offer in their art what Michael Longley has called 'the sacraments we invent for ourselves'.

We are no longer innocent, we are no longer just parishioners of the local. We go to Paris at Easter instead of rolling eggs on the hill at the gable. 'Chicken Marengo! It's a far cry from the Moy', Paul Muldoon says in a line depth-charged with architectural history. Yet those primary laws of our nature are still operative. We are dwellers, we are namers, we are lovers, we make homes and search for our histories. And when we look for the history of our sensibilities I am convinced, as Professor J. C. Beckett was convinced about the history of Ireland generally, that it is to what he called the stable element, the land itself, that we must look for continuity.

Lecture given in the Ulster Museum, January 1977

Englands of the Mind

One of the most precise and suggestive of T. S. Eliot's critical
formulations was his notion of what he called 'the auditory
imagination', 'the feeling for syllable and rhythm, penetrating
far below the conscious levels of thought and feeling, invigorat-
ing every word; sinking to the most primitive and forgotten,
returning to the origin and bringing something back', fusing
'the most ancient and the most civilized mentality'. I presume
Eliot was thinking here about the cultural depth-charges latent
in certain words and rhythms, that binding secret between
words in poetry that delights not just the ear but the whole
backward and abysm of mind and body; thinking of the energies beating in and between words that the poet brings into
half-deliberate play; thinking of the relationship between the
word as pure vocable, as articulate noise, and the word as
etymological occurrence, as symptom of human history,
memory and attachments.

It is in the context of this auditory imagination that I wish to
discuss the language of Ted Hughes, Geoffrey Hill and Philip
Larkin. All of them return to an origin and bring something
back, all three live off the hump of the English poetic achievement, all three, here and now, in England, imply a continuity
with another England, there and then. All three are hoarders
and shorers of what they take to be the real England. All three
treat England as a region—or rather treat their region as
England—in different and complementary ways. I believe they
are afflicted with a sense of history that was once the peculiar
affliction of the poets of other nations who were not themselves
natives of England but who spoke the English language. The
poets of the mother culture, I feel, are now possessed of that
defensive love of their territory which was once shared only by

those poets whom we might call colonial—Yeats, MacDiarmid, Carlos Williams. They are aware of their Englishness as deposits in the descending storeys of the literary and historical past. Their very terrain is becoming consciously precious. A desire to preserve indigenous traditions, to keep open the imagination's supply lines to the past, to receive from the stations of Anglo-Saxon confirmations of ancestry, to perceive in the rituals of show Saturdays and race-meetings and seaside outings, of church-going and marriages at Whitsun, and in the necessities that crave expression after the ritual of church-going has passed away, to perceive in these a continuity of communal ways, and a confirmation of an identity which is threatened—all this is signified by their language.

When we examine that language, we find that their three separate voices are guaranteed by three separate foundations which, when combined, represent almost the total resources of the English language itself. Hughes relies on the northern deposits, the pagan Anglo-Saxon and Norse elements, and he draws energy also from a related constellation of primitive myths and world views. The life of his language is a persistence of the stark outline and vitality of Anglo-Saxon that became the Middle English alliterative tradition and then went underground to sustain the folk poetry, the ballads, and the ebullience of Shakespeare and the Elizabethans. Hill is also sustained by the Anglo-Saxon base, but his proper guarantor is that language as modified and amplified by the vocabularies and values of the Mediterranean, by the early medieval Latin influence; his is to a certain extent a scholastic imagination founded on an England that we might describe as Anglo-Romanesque, touched by the polysyllabic light of Christianity but possessed by darker energies which might be acknowledged as barbaric. Larkin then completes the picture, because his proper hinterland is the English language Frenchified and turned humanist by the Norman conquest and the Renaissance, made nimble, melodious and plangent by Chaucer and Spenser, and besomed clean of its inkhornisms and its irrational magics by the eighteenth century.

And their Englands of the mind might be correspondingly characterized. Hughes's is a primeval landscape where stones cry out and horizons endure, where the elements inhabit the mind with a religious force, where the pebble dreams 'it is the foetus of God', 'where the staring angels go through', 'where all the stars bow down', where, with appropriately pre-Socratic force, water lies 'at the bottom of all things/utterly worn out utterly clear'. It is England as King Lear's heath which now becomes a Yorkshire moor where sheep and foxes and hawks persuade 'unaccommodated man' that he is a poor bare forked thing, kinned not in a chain but on a plane of being with the animals themselves. There monoliths and lintels. The air is menaced by God's voice in the wind, by demonic protean crow-shapes; and the poet is a wanderer among the ruins, cut off by catastrophe from consolation and philosophy. Hill's England, on the other hand, is more hospitable to the human presence. The monoliths make way for the keeps and chantries if also for the beheading block. The heath's loneliness is kept at bay by the natural magic of the grove and the intellectual force of the scholar's cell. The poet is not a wanderer but a clerk or perhaps an illuminator or one of a guild of masters: he is in possession of a history rather than a mythology; he has a learned rather than an oral tradition. There are wars, but there are also dynasties, ideas of inheritance and order, possibilities for the 'true governaunce of England'. His elegies are not laments for the irrevocable dispersal of the *comitatus* and the ring-giver in the hall, but solemn requiems for Plantagenet kings whose murderous wars are set in a great pattern, to be understood only when 'the sea/Across daubed rocks evacuates its dead'. And Larkin's England similarly reflects features from the period that his language is hived off. His trees and flowers and grasses are neither animistic, nor hallowed by half-remembered druidic lore; they are emblems of mutabilitie. Behind them lies the sensibility of troubadour and courtier. 'Cut grass lies frail;/ Brief is the breath/Mown stalks exhale'; his landscape is dominated neither by the untamed heath nor the totemistic architectures of spire and battlement but by the civic prospects, by roofs and gardens and prospects where urban and pastoral visions interact as 'postal districts packed like squares of wheat'. The poet is no longer a bardic remnant nor an initiate in curious learning nor a jealous master of the secrets of a craft; he is a humane and civilized member of the customs service or the civil service or, indeed, the library service. The moon is no longer

152

his white goddess but his poetic property, to be image rather than icon: 'high and preposterous and separate', she watches over unfenced existence, over fulfilment's desolate attic, over an England of department stores, canals and floatings of industrial froth, explosions in mines, effigies in churches, secretaries in offices; and she hauls tides of life where only one ship is worth celebration, not a Golden Hind or a Victory, but 'black-/Sailed unfamiliar, towing at her back/A huge and birdless silence.'

Hughes's sensibility is pagan in the original sense: he is a haunter of the *pagus*, a heath-dweller, a heathen; he moves by instinct in the thickets beyond the *urbs*; he is neither urban nor urbane. His poetry is as redolent of the lair as it is of the library. The very titles of his books are casts made into the outback of our animal recognitions. *Lupercal*, a word infested with wolfish stinks yet returning to an origin in Shakespeare's *Julius Caesar*: 'You all did see that on the Lupercal/I thrice presented him a kingly crown.' Yet the word passes back through Shakespeare into the Lupercal, a cave below the western corner of the Palatine Hill in Rome; and the Lupercal was also the festival held on 15 February when, after the sacrifice of goats and a dog, youths dressed only in girdles made from the skins of these victims ran about the bounds of the Palatine city, striking those whom they met, especially women, with strips of goatskin. It was a fertility rite, and it was also a ritual beating of the bounds of the city, and in a way Hughes's language is just this also. Its sensuous fetch, its redolence of blood and gland and grass and water, recalled English poetry in the fifties from a too suburban aversion of the attention from the elemental; and the poems beat the bounds of a hidden England in streams and trees, on moors and in byres. Hughes appeared like Poor Tom on the heath, a civilized man tasting and testing the primitive facts; he appeared as *Wodwo*, a nosing wild man of the woods. The volume *Wodwo* appeared in 1967 and carried as its epigraph a quotation from *Gawain and the Green Knight*, and that deliberate affiliation is instructive. Like the art of Gawain, Hughes's art is one of clear outline and inner richness. His diction is consonantal, and it snicks through the air like an efficient blade, marking and carving out fast definite shapes; but within those shapes, mysteries and rituals

153

are hinted at. They are circles within which he conjures up presences.

Hughes's vigour has much to do with this matter of consonants that take the measure of his vowels like calipers, or stud the line like rivets. 'Everything is inheriting everything,' as he says in one of his poems, and what he has inherited through Shakespeare and John Webster and Hopkins and Lawrence is something of that primary life of stress which is the quick of the English poetic matter. His consonants are the Norsemen, the Normans, the Roundheads in the world of his vocables, hacking and hedging and hammering down the abundance and luxury and possible lasciviousness of the vowels. 'I imagine this midnight moment's forest'—the first line of the well-known 'The Thought Fox'—is hushed, but it is a hush achieved by the quelling, battening-down action of the m's and d's and t's: I iMagine this MiDnighT MoMenT's foresT. Hughes's aspiration in these early poems is to command all the elements, to bring them within the jurisdiction of his authoritarian voice. And in 'The Thought Fox' the thing at the beginning of the poem which lives beyond his jurisdiction is characteristically fluid and vowelling and sibilant: 'Something else is alive' whispers of a presence not yet accounted for, a presence that is granted its full vowel music as its epiphany—'Something more near/Though deeper within darkness/Is entering the loneliness.' It is granted this dilation of its mystery before it is conjured into the possession of the poet-warden, the vowelkeeper; and its final emergence in the fully sounded i's and e's of 'an eye,/A widening deepening greenness,' is gradually mastered by the braking action of 'brilliantly, concentratedly', and by the shooting of the monosyllabic consonantal bolts in the last stanza:

> Till, with a sudden sharp hot stink of fox
> It enters the dark hole of the head.
> The window is starless still; the clock ticks,
> The page is printed.

Next a poem whose subject might be expected to woo the tender pious vowels from a poet rather than the disciplining consonants. About a 'Fern':

> Here is the fern's frond, unfurling a gesture,

154

The first line is an Anglo-Saxon line, four stresses, three of
them picked out by alliteration; and although the frosty grip of
those f's thaws out, the fern is still subsumed into images of
control and discipline and regal authority:

> And, among them, the fern
> Dances gravely, like the plume
> Of a warrior returning, under the low hills,
>
> Into his own kingdom.

But of course we recognize that Hughes's 'Thistles' are vegetation more kindred to his spirit than the pliant fern. And when he
turns his attention to them, they become reincarnations of the
Norsemen in a poem entitled 'The Warriors of the North':

> Bringing their frozen swords, their salt-bleached eyes, their salt-
> bleached hair,
> The snow's stupefied anvils in rows,
> Bringing their envy,
> The slow ships feelered Southward, snails over the steep sheen of
> the water-globe

and he imagines them resurrected in all their arctic mail 'into
the iron arteries of Calvin', and into 'Thistles'. The thistles are
emblems of the Hughes voice as I see it, born of an original
vigour, fighting back over the same ground; and it is not
insignificant that in this poem Hughes himself imagines the
thistles as images of a fundamental speech, uttering itself in
gutturals from behind the sloped arms of consonants:

> Every one a revengeful burst
> Of resurrection, a grasped fistful
> Of splintered weapons and Icelandic frost thrust up
>
> From the underground stain of a decayed Viking.
> They are like pale hair and the gutturals of dialects.
> Every one manages a plume of blood.
>
> Then they grow grey, like men.
> Mown down, it is a feud. Their sons appear,
> Stiff with weapons, fighting back over the same ground.

The gutturals of dialects, which Hughes here connects with the
Nordic stratum of English speech, he pronounces in another

place to be the germinal secret of his own voice. In an interview published in the *London Magazine* in January 1971 he said:

> I grew up in West Yorkshire. They have a very distinctive dialect there. Whatever other speech you grow into, presumably your dialect stays alive in a sort of inner freedom, . . . it's your childhood self there inside the dialect and that is possibly your real self or the core of it. . . . Without it, I doubt if I would ever have written verse. And in the case of the West Yorkshire dialect, of course, it connects you directly and in your most intimate self to Middle English poetry.

In other words he finds that the original grain of his speech is a chip off the old block and that his work need not be a new planting but a new bud on an old bough. What other poet would have the boldness to entitle a collection *Wodwo*? Yet *Gawain and the Green Knight*, with its beautiful alliterating and illuminated form, its interlacing and trellising of natural life and mythic life, is probably closer in spirit to Hughes's poetry than Hughes's poetry is to that of his English contemporaries. Everything inherits everything—and Hughes is the rightful heir to this alliterative tradition, and to the cleaving simplicity of the Border ballad, which he elevates to the status of touchstone later in that same interview. He says that he started writing again in 1955:

> The poems that set me off were odd pieces by Shapiro, Lowell, Merwin, Wilbur and Crowe Ransom. Crowe Ransom was the one who gave me a model I felt I could use. He helped me get my words into focus. . . . But this whole business of influences is mysterious. . . . And after all the campaigns to make it new you're stuck with the fact that some of the Scots Border ballads still cut a deeper groove than anything written in the last forty years. Influences just seem to make it more and more unlikely that a poet will write what he alone could write.

What Hughes alone could write depended for its release on the discovery of a way to undam the energies of the dialect, to get a stomping ground for that inner freedom, to get that childhood self a disguise to roam at large in. Freedom and naturalness and homeliness are positives in Hughes's critical vocabulary, and they are linked with both the authenticity of individual poets and the genius of the language itself. Speaking of Keith Douglas in 1964, Hughes could have been speaking of himself; of the way his language and his imagination alerted themselves when the hunt for the poem in the adult world became synonymous with the hunt for the animal in the world of childhood, the world of dialect:

> The impression is of a sudden mobilizing of the poet's will, a clearing of his vision, as if from sitting considering possibilities and impossibilities he stood up to act. Pictures of things no longer interest him much: he wants their substance, their nature and their consequences in life. At once, and quite suddenly, his mind is whole.... He is a renovator of language. It is not that he uses words in jolting combinations, or with titanic extravagance, or curious precision. His triumph is in the way he renews the simplicity of ordinary talk.... The music that goes along with this ... is the natural path of such confident, candid thinking.... A utility general purpose style that combines a colloquial prose readiness with poetic breadth, a ritual intensity of music with clear direct feeling, and yet in the end is nothing but casual speech.

This combination of ritual intensity, prose readiness, direct feeling and casual speech can be discovered likewise in the best poems of *Lupercal*, because in *Hawk in the Rain* and indeed in much of *Wodwo* and *Crow*, we are often in the presence of that titanic extravagance Hughes mentions, speech not so much mobilizing and standing up to act as flexing and straining until it verges on the grotesque. But in poems like 'Pike', 'Hawk Roosting', 'The Bull Moses' and 'An Otter' we get this confident, speedy, hammer-and-tongs proficiency. And in this poem from *Wodwo*, called 'Pibroch', a poem uniquely Hughesian in its very title, fetching energy and ancestry from what is beyond the Pale and beneath the surface, we have the elements of the Scottish piper's *ceol mor*, the high style, implicit in words like 'dead', 'heaven', 'universe', 'aeon', 'angels', and in phrases like 'the foetus of God', 'the stars bow down'—a phrase which cunningly makes its cast and raises Blake in the pool of the ear. We have elements of this high style, ritual intensity, whatever you want to call it; and we have also the 'prose readiness', the 'casual speech' of 'bored', 'hangs on', 'lets up', 'tryout', and the workaday cadences of 'Over the stone rushes the wind', and 'her mind's gone completely'. The landscape of the poem is one that the Anglo-Saxon wanderer or seafarer would be completely at home in:

> The sea cries with its meaningless voice
> Treating alike its dead and its living,
> Probably bored with the appearance of heaven
> After so many millions of nights without sleep,
> Without purpose, without self-deception.
>
> Stone likewise. A pebble is imprisoned
> Like nothing in the Universe.
> Created for black sleep. Or growing
> Conscious of the sun's red spot occasionally,
> Then dreaming it is the foetus of God.
>
> Over the stone rushes the wind
> Able to mingle with nothing,
> Like the hearing of the blind stone itself.
> Or turns, as if the stone's mind came feeling
> A fantasy of directions.
>
> Drinking the sea and eating the rock
> A tree struggles to make leaves—
> An old woman fallen from space
> Unprepared for these conditions.
> She hangs on, because her mind's gone completely.
>
> Minute after minute, aeon after aeon,
> Nothing lets up or develops.
> And this is neither a bad variant nor a tryout.
> This is where the staring angels go through.
> This is where all the stars bow down.

Hughes attempts to make vocal the inner life, the simple being-thereness, 'the substance, nature and consequences in life' of sea, stone, wind and tree. Blake's pebble and tiger are shadowy presences in the background, as are the landscapes of Anglo-Saxon poetry. And the whole thing is founded on rock, that rock which Hughes presented in his autobiographical essay as his birthstone, holding his emergence in place just as his headstone will hold his decease:

> This was the *memento mundi* over my birth: my spiritual midwife at the time and my godfather ever since—or one of my godfathers.

From my first day it watched. If it couldn't see me direct, a towering gloom over my pram, it watched me through a species of periscope: that is, by infiltrating the very light of my room with its particular shadow. From my home near the bottom of the south-facing slope of the valley, the cliff was both the curtain and back-drop to existence.

I quote this piece because it links the childhood core with the adult opus, because that rock is the equivalent in his poetic landscape of dialect in his poetic speech. The rock persists, survives, sustains, endures and informs his imagination, just as it is the bedrock of the language upon which Hughes founds his version of survival and endurance.

Stone and rock figure prominently in the world of Geoffrey Hill's poetry also, but Hill's imagination is not content to grant the mineral world the absolute sway that Hughes allows it. He is not the suppliant chanting to the megalith, but rather the mason dressing it. Hill also beats the bounds of an England, his own native West Midlands, beheld as a medieval England facing into the Celtic mysteries of Wales and out towards the military and ecclesiastical splendours of Europe. His *Mercian Hymns* names his territory Mercia, and masks his imagination under the figure of King Offa, builder of Offa's dyke between England and Wales, builder as well as beater of the boundaries. Hill's cele-bration of Mercia has a double-focus: one a child's-eye view, close to the common earth, the hoard of history, and the other the historian's and scholar's eye, inquisitive of meaning, bring-ing time past to bear on time present and vice versa. But the writing itself is by no means abstract and philosophical. Hill addresses the language, as I say, like a mason addressing a block, not unlike his own mason in Hymn XXIV:

Itinerant through numerous domains, of his lord's retinue, to Compostela. Then home for a lifetime amid West Mercia this master-mason as I envisage him, intent to pester upon tym-panum and chancel-arch his moody testament, confusing war-rior with lion, dragon-coils, tendrils of the stony vine.

Where best to stand? Easter sunrays catch the oblique face of Adam scrumping through leaves; pale spree of evangelists and, there, a cross Christ mumming child Adam out of Hell

159

('Et exspecto resurrectionem mortuorum' dust in the eyes, on
clawing wings, and lips)

Not only must English be kept up here, with its 'spree' and
'scrumping' and 'mumming', but Latin and learning must be
kept up too. The mannered rhetoric of these pieces is a kind of
verbal architecture, a grave and sturdy English Romanesque.
The native undergrowth, both vegetative and verbal, that barbaric scrollwork of fern and ivy, is set against the tympanum
and chancel-arch, against the weighty elegance of imperial
Latin. The overall pattern of his language is an extension and a
deliberate exploitation of the linguistic effect in Shakespeare's
famous lines, 'It would the multitudinous seas incarnadine,/
Making the green one red,' where the polysyllabic flourish of
'multitudinous' and 'incarnadine' is both set off and undercut
by the monosyllabic plainness of 'making the green one red',
where the Latinate and the local also go hand in glove. There is
in Hill something of Stephen Dedalus's hyperconsciousness of
words as physical sensations, as sounds to be plumbed, as
weights on the tongue. Words in his poetry fall slowly and
singly, like molten solder, and accumulate to a dull glowing
nub. I imagine Hill as indulging in a morose linguistic delec-
tation, dwelling on the potential of each word with much the
same slow relish as Leopold Bloom dwells on the thought of his
kidney. And in *Mercian Hymns*, in fact, Hill's procedure resembles Joyce's not only in this linguistic deliberation and self-
consciousness. For all his references to the 'precedent provided
by the Latin prose-hymns or canticles of the early Christian
Church', what these hymns celebrate is the 'ineluctable modality of the audible', as well as the visible, and the form that
celebration takes reminds one of the Joycean epiphany, which is
a prose poem in effect. But not only in the form of the individual
pieces, but in the overall structuring of the pieces, he follows
the Joycean precedent set in *Ulysses* of confounding modern
autobiographical material with literary and historic matter
drawn from the past. Offa's story makes contemporary landscape and experience live in the rich shadows of a tradition.

To go back to Hymn XXIV, the occasion, the engendering
moment, seems to involve the contemplation of a carved pedi-
ment—a tympanum is the carved area between the lintel of a

door and the arch above it—which exhibits a set of scenes: one of Eden, one of some kind of harrowing of hell; and the scenes are supervised by images of the evangelists. And this cryptic, compressed mode of presentation in which a few figures on stone can call upon the whole body of Christian doctrines and mythology resembles the compression of the piece itself. The carving reminds him of the carver, a master-mason—and the relevant note reads: 'for the association of Compostela with West Midlands sculpture of the twelfth century I am indebted to G. Zarnecki, *Later English Romanesque Sculpture*, London (1953).' This mason is 'itinerant'—a word used in its precise Latin sense, yet when applied to a travelling craftsman, that pristine sense seems to foreshadow its present narrowed meaning of tinker, a travelling tinsmith, a white-smith. In the first phrases the Latinate predominates, for this is a ritual progress, an itinerary 'through numerous domains, of his lord's retinue', to Compostela. Even the proper name flaps out its music like some banner there. But when he gets home, he is momentarily cut down from his grand tour importance to his homely size, in the simple 'Then home for a lifetime amid West Mercia'; but now the poet/observer of the carving has caught something of the sense of occasion and borrowed something of the mason's excitement. Yet he does not 'see in the mind's eye', like Hamlet, but 'envisages' him, the verb being properly liturgical, 'intent to pester upon tympanum and chancel-arch his moody testament, confusing warrior with lion, dragon-coils . . .' Tympanum, of course, is also a drum, and the verb 'pester' manages a rich synaesthetic effect; the stone is made to cackle like a kettle drum as the chisel hits it. But 'pester' is more interesting still. Its primary meaning, from the original Latin root, *pastorium*, means to hobble a horse, and it was used in 1685 to mean 'crowding persons in or into'. So the mason hobbles and herds and crowds in warrior and lion, dragon coils, tendrils of the stony vine; and this interlacing and entanglement of motifs is also the method of the poem.

In fact, we can see the method more clearly if we put the poem in its proper context, which is in the middle of a group of three entitled *Opus Anglicanum*. Once again the note is helpful:

'*Opus Anglicanum*': the term is properly applicable to English embroidery of the period AD 1250–1350, though the craft was already famous some centuries earlier.... I have, with considerable impropriety, extended the term to apply to English Romanesque sculpture and to utilitarian metal-work of the nineteenth century.

The entanglement, the interlacing, is now that of embroidery, and this first poem, I suggest, brings together womanly figures from Hill's childhood memory with the ghostly procession of needleworkers from the medieval castles and convents:

XXIII

In tapestries, in dreams, they gathered, as it was enacted, the return, the re-entry of transcendence into this sublunary world. *Opus Anglicanum*, their stringent mystery riddled by needles: the silver veining, the gold leaf, voluted grape-vine, masterworks of treacherous thread.

They trudged out of the dark, scraping their boots free from lime-splodges and phlegm. They munched cold bacon. The lamps grew plump with oily reliable light.

Again, the liturgical and Latinate of the first paragraph is abraded and rebutted by the literal and local weight of 'scraping their boots free from lime-splodges and phlegm'—the boots being, I take it, the boots of labourers involved in this never-ending *Opus Anglicanum*, from agricultural origins to industrial developments. And in order just to clinch the thing, consider the third piece, where the 'utilitarian iron work' in which his grandmother was involved is contemplated in a perspective that includes medieval embroidress and mason, and a certain 'transcendence' enters the making of wire nails:

XXV

Brooding on the eightieth letter of *Fors Clavigera*, I speak this in memory of my grandmother, whose childhood and prime womanhood were spent in the nailer's darg.

The nailshop stood back of the cottage, by the fold. It reeked stale mineral sweat. Sparks had furred its low roof. In dawn-light the troughed water floated a damson-bloom of dust—

not to be shaken by posthumous clamour. It is one thing to celebrate the 'quick forge', another to cradle a face hare-lipped by the searing wire.

> Brooding on the eightieth letter of *Fors Clavigera*, I speak this in
> memory of my grandmother, whose childhood and prime
> womanhood were spent in the nailer's darg.

Ruskin's eightieth letter reflects eloquently and plangently on
the injustice of the master and servant situation, on the exploitation of labour, on the demeaning work in a nail forge. The
Mayor of Birmingham took him to a house where two women
were at work, labouring, as he says, with ancient Vulcanian
skill:

> So wrought they,—the English matron and maid;—so it was their
> darg to labour from morning to evening—seven to seven—by the
> furnace side—the winds of summer fanning the blast of it.

He goes on to compute that the woman and the husband earn
altogether £55 a year with which to feed and clothe themselves
and their six children, to reproach the luxury of the mill-owning
class, and to compare the wives of industrialists contemplating
Burne Jones's picture of Venus's mirror 'with these, their sis-
ters, who had only, for Venus's mirror, a heap of ashes;
compassed about with no forget-me-nots, but with all the
forgetfulness in the world'.

It seems to me here that Hill is celebrating his own indomit-
able Englishry, casting his mind on other days, singing a clan
beaten into the clay and ashes, and linking their patience, their
sustaining energy, with the glory of England. The 'quick forge',
after all, may be what its origin in Shakespeare's *Henry V*
declares it to be, 'the quick forge and working house of thought',
but it is surely also the 'random grim forge' of Felix Randal, the
farrier. The image shifts between various points and
embroiders a new *opus anglicanum* in this intended and allusive
poem. And the point of the embroidering needle, of course, is
darg, that chip off the Anglo-Saxon block, meaning 'a day's
work, or the task of a day'.

The *Mercian Hymns* show Hill in full command of his voice.
Much as the stiff and corbelled rhetoric of earlier work like
Funeral Music and 'Requiem for the Plantagenet Kings' stands
up and will stand up, it is only when this rhetoric becomes a
press tightening on and squeezing out of the language the
vigour of common speech, the essential Anglo-Saxon juices, it
is only then that the poetry attains this final refreshed and

refreshing quality: then he has, in the words of another piece, accrued a 'golden and stinking blaze'.

Finally, to come to Larkin, where what accrues in the language is not 'a golden and stinking blaze', not the rank and fermenting composts of philology and history, but the bright senses of words worn clean in literate conversation. In Larkin's language as in his vision of water, 'any angled light ... congregate[s] endlessly.' There is a gap in Larkin between the perceiver and the thing perceived, a refusal to melt through long perspectives, an obstinate insistence that the poet is neither a race memory nor a myth-kitty nor a mason, but a real man in a real place. The cadences and vocabulary of his poems are tuned to a rational music. It would seem that he has deliberately curtailed his gift for evocation, for resonance, for symbolist *frissons*. He turned from Yeats to Hardy as his master. He never followed the Laurentian success of his early poem 'Wedding Wind' which ends with a kind of biblical swoon, an image of fulfilled lovers 'kneeling like cattle by all generous waters'. He rebukes romantic aspiration and afflatus with a scrupulous meanness. If he sees the moon, he sees it while groping back to bed after a piss. If he is forced to cry out 'O wolves of memory, immensements', he is also forced to recognize that he is past all that swaddling of sentiment, even if it is 'for others, undiminished, somewhere'. 'Undiminished'—the word, with its hovering balance between attenuated possibilities and the possibility of amplitude, is typical. And Christopher Ricks has pointed out how often negatives operate in Larkin's best lines. Lovers talking in bed, for example, discover it ever more difficult

> to find
> Words at once true and kind,
> Or not untrue and not unkind.

His tongue moves hesitantly, precisely, honestly, among ironies and negatives. He is the poet of rational light, a light that has its own luminous beauty but which has also the effect of exposing clearly the truths which it touches. Larkin speaks neither a dialect nor a pulpit language; there are no 'hectoring large scale verses' in his three books, nor is there the stubbly intimacy of 'oath-edged talk and pipe-smoke' which he nostalgically annotates among the miners. His language would have pleased those Tudor and Augustan guardians who wanted to polish and beautify their speech, to smooth it for art. What we hear is a stripped standard English voice, a voice indeed with a unique break and remorseful tone, but a voice that leads back neither to the thumping beat of Anglo-Saxon nor to the Gregorian chant of the Middle Ages. Its ancestry begins, in fact, when the Middle Ages are turning secular, and plays begin to take their place beside the Mass as a form of communal telling and knowing. In the first few lines of Larkin's poem 'Money', for example, I think I hear the cadences of *Everyman*, the querulous tones of Riches reproaching the hero:

> Quarterly, is it, money reproaches me:
> 'Why do you let me lie here wastefully?
> I am all you never had of goods and sex.
> You could get them still just by writing a few cheques.'

Those endstopped lines, sliding down to rhymed conclusions, suggest the beginning of that period out of which Larkin's style arises. After *Everyman*, there is Skelton, a common-sensical wobble of rhyme, a humorous wisdom, a practical lyricism:

> Oh, no one can deny
> That Arnold is less selfish than I.
> He married a wife to stop her getting away
> Now she's there all day, . . .

There is as well the Cavalier Larkin, the maker of songs, where the conversational note and the dainty disciplines of a metrical form are in beautiful equilibrium:

> Yet still the unresting castles thresh
> In fullgrown thickness every May.
> Last year is dead, they seem to say.
> Begin afresh, afresh, afresh.

Even in that short space, by the way, one can see the peculiar Larkin fusion of parsimony and abundance—the gorgeousness of 'unresting castles', the poignant sweetness of 'afresh, afresh' are held in check by the quotidian 'last year is dead'. Yet it is by refusing to pull out the full stops, or by almost refusing, that Larkin gains his own brand of negative capability.

As well as the Cavalier Larkin, there is a late Augustan Larkin, the poet of decorous melancholy moods, of twilit propriety and shadowy melody. His poem about superannuated racehorses, for example, entitled 'At Grass', could well be subtitled, 'An Elegy in a Country Paddock'. Behind the trees where the horses shelter there could well rise the spire of Stoke Poges church; and behind the smooth numbers of wind distressing the tails and manes, there is the donnish exactitude of tresses being *dis*tressed:

> The eye can hardly pick them out
> From the cold shade they shelter in
> Till wind distresses tail and mane ...

And when, at the conclusion of the poem, 'the groom and the groom's boy/With bridles in the evening come,' their footsteps surely echo the ploughman homeward plodding his weary way.

There is, moreover, a Tennysonian Larkin and a Hardyesque Larkin. There is even, powerfully, an Imagist Larkin:

> There is an evening coming in
> Across the fields, one never seen before,
> That lights no lamps.
>
> Silken it seems at a distance, yet
> When it is drawn up over the knees and breast
> It brings no comfort.
>
> Where has the tree gone, that locked
> Earth to the sky? What is under my hands,
> That I cannot feel?
>
> What loads my hands down?

Then there is Larkin, the coiner of compounds—which we may choose to call Hopkinsian or even perhaps, briefly, Shakespearean—who writes of 'some lonely rain-ceased midsummer evening', of 'light unanswerable and tall and wide', of 'the million-petalled flower of being here', of 'thin continuous dreaming' and 'wasteful, weak, propitiatory flowers'.

And to go from the sublime to the ridiculous, there is the seaside-postcard Larkin, as true to the streak of vulgarity in the civilization as he is sensitive to its most delicious refinements:

'Get stewed:/Books are a load of crap.' Or get this disfigure-
ment of a poster of a bathing beauty:

> Huge tits and a fissured crotch
> Were scored well in, and the space
> Between her legs held scrawls
> That set her fairly astride
> A tuberous cock and balls.

And then, elsewhere,

> They fuck you up, your mum and dad.
> They may not mean to but they do.
> They fill you with the faults they had
> And add some extra, just for you.

And again, in 'Sad Steps':

> Groping back to bed after a piss
> I part thick curtains, and am startled by
> The rapid clouds, the moon's cleanliness.

But despite the piss, and the snigger of the demotic in all of
these places, that title, 'Sad Steps', reminds us that Larkin is
solicitous for his Sidney also. He too returns to origins and
brings something back, although he does not return to 'roots'.
He puts inverted commas round his 'roots', in fact. His childhood, he says, was a forgotten boredom. He sees England from
train windows, fleeting past and away. He is urban modern
man, the insular Englishman, responding to the tones of his
own clan, ill at ease when out of his environment. He is a poet,
indeed, of composed and tempered English nationalism, and
his voice is the not untrue, not unkind voice of post-war
England, where the cloth cap and the royal crown have both lost
some of their potent symbolism, and the categorical, socially
defining functions of the working-class accent and the aristocratic drawl have almost been eroded. Larkin's tones are
mannerly but not exquisite, well-bred but not mealy-mouthed.
If his England and his English are not as deep as Hughes's or as
solemn as Hill's, they are nevertheless dearly beloved, and
during his sojourn in Belfast in the late fifties, he gave thanks,
by implication, for the nurture that he receives by living among
his own. The speech, the customs, the institutions of England
are, in the words of another English poet, domiciled in Ireland,

167

'wife to his creating thought'. That was Hopkins in Dublin in the 1880s, sensing that his individual talent was being divorced from his tradition. Here is Larkin remembering the domicile in Belfast in the 1950s:

> Lonely in Ireland, since it was not home,
> Strangeness made sense. The salt rebuff of speech,
> Insisting so on difference, made me welcome:
> Once that was recognised, we were in touch.
>
> Their draughty streets, end-on to hills, the faint
> Archaic smell of dockland, like a stable,
> The herring-hawker's cry, dwindling, went
> To prove me separate, not unworkable.
>
> Living in England has no such excuse:
> These are my customs and establishments
> It would be much more serious to refuse.
> Here no elsewhere underwrites my existence.

Larkin's England of the mind is in many ways continuous with the England of Rupert Brooke's 'Grantchester' and Edward Thomas's 'Adlestrop', an England of customs and institutions, industrial and domestic, but also an England whose pastoral hinterland is threatened by the very success of those institutions. Houses and roads and factories mean that a certain England is 'Going, Going':

> It seems, just now,
> To be happening so very fast;
> Despite all the land left free
> For the first time I feel somehow
> That it isn't going to last,
>
> That before I snuff it, the whole
> Boiling will be bricked in
> Except for the tourist parts—
> First slum of Europe: a role
> It won't be so hard to win,
> With a cast of crooks and tarts.
>
> And that will be England gone,
> The shadows, the meadows, the lanes,
> The guildhalls, the carved choirs.

There'll be books; it will linger on
In galleries; but all that remains
For us will be concrete and tyres.

I think that sense of an ending has driven all three of these writers into a kind of piety towards their local origins, has made them look in, rather than up, to England. The loss of imperial power, the failure of economic nerve, the diminished influence of Britain inside Europe, all this has led to a new sense of the shires, a new valuing of the native English experience. Donald Davie, for example, has published a book of poems, with that very title, *The Shires*, which attempts to annex to his imagination by personal memory or historical meditation or literary connections, each shire of England. It is a book at once intimate and exclusive, a topography of love and impatience, and it is yet another symptom that English poets are being forced to explore not just the matter of England, but what is the matter with England. I have simply presumed to share in that exploration through the medium which England has, for better or worse, impressed upon us all, the English language itself.

The Beckman Lecture, given at the University of
California, Berkeley, May 1976

III

In the Country of Convention

*English Pastoral Verse**

'Pastoral' is a term that has been extended by usage until its original meaning has been largely eroded. For example, I have occasionally talked of the countryside where we live in Wicklow as being pastoral rather than rural, trying to impose notions of a beautified landscape on the word, in order to keep 'rural' for the unselfconscious face of raggle-taggle farmland. And we have been hearing about Hardy and Hemingway as writers of pastoral novels, which seems a satisfactory categorization. Originally, of course, the word means 'of or pertaining to shepherds or their occupation' and hence 'a poem, play, etc, in which the life of shepherds is portrayed, often in conventional manner: also extended to works dealing with country life generally.'

The editors of *The Penguin Book of English Pastoral Verse* have stayed within the limits set by the dictionary, and have confined themselves, in their choice of verse from the Romantic period and later, to those 'works dealing with country life' which refract the pastoral convention as it manifests itself in the English poetic tradition from the late sixteenth until the eighteenth century. Consequently, there is a relatively small showing of nineteenth-century work, and only three poems by writers who can be considered modern: one each by Hopkins, Hardy and Yeats. The bulk of the work comes from the seventeenth and eighteenth centuries, and the editors end their introduction with a sentence that drops like a portcullis:

*John Barrell and John Bull (eds.), *The Penguin Book of English Pastoral Verse*, Allen Lane, 1975.

173

The Pastoral vision might still have life elsewhere—in the Third World, or in North America perhaps—where there are still occasional frontiers to confront the regulating effect of urban development; but now and in England, the Pastoral, occasional twitches notwithstanding, is a lifeless form, of service only to decorate the shelves of tasteful cottages, 'modernized to a high standard'.

The anthology, then, could be subtitled 'the rise and fall of the pastoral convention in England'. It is a packed and well-groomed book, not so much a region to wander in as an estate to be guided through, and John Barrell and John Bull are always intent on being a little ahead of us, to make sure that we see the ground from their point of view. They divide the book into seven sections, each with its separate introduction, which means that we are given a brief history of the form in seven short chapters, dealing consecutively with 'The Elizabethan Pastoral', 'The Pastoral Drama', 'The Seventeenth-Century Pastoral', 'Augustan Pastoral', 'Whigs and Post-Augustans', 'Some Versions of Anti-Pastoral', and 'Romantics and Victorians'.

Through all this, the editors' approach is consistent to the point of being, in the end, constricting. They insist that

> the pastoral vision is, at base, a false vision, positing a simplistic, unhistorical relationship between the ruling landowning class—the poet's patrons and often the poet himself—and the workers of the land; as such its function is to mystify and to obscure the harshness of actual social and economic organization.

This is the approach elaborated by Raymond Williams in *The Country and the City* and to a certain extent this book is a companion volume to Mr. Williams's, incorporating most of the texts he refers to and underlining or extending his discussion of them. Now this sociological filleting of the convention is a bracing corrective to an over-literary savouring of it as a matter of classical imitation and allusion, but it nevertheless entails a certain attenuation of response, so that consideration of the selected poems as made things, as self-delighting buds on the old bough of a tradition, is much curtailed. The Marxist broom sweeps the poetic enterprise clean of those somewhat hedonistic impulses towards the satisfactions of aural and formal play out of which poems arise, whether they aspire to delineate or to obfuscate 'things as they are'.

In spite of the assent which their thesis earns, and gratitude for the abundance of material with which it is illustrated, the value of the book seems to me to be lessened by the editors' decision not to print translations of Theocritus, Virgil, Horace, Mantuan, Marot—those informing, influencing voices that were 'modified in the guts of the living'. While there was indeed mystification (a word I am reluctant to regard as *altogether* pejorative in poetry) of economic and social realities in Renaissance and eighteenth-century pastoral, there was surely also the purely literary ambition to provide a poetry in English that would adorn and classicize the native literature. Spenser, Milton, Pope and Thomson were as automatically conscious of the classical penumbra behind their own efforts as most of today's students are unconscious of it, and since this book is likely to attain textbook status it is a pity that the ancient hinterland, the perspectives backward, are withheld.

We begin, therefore, in the middle of things English, with Barnabe Googe, Sidney, Spenser, Raleigh and Drayton. It is impossible to miss the note both of exhilaration and consolidation in this work as English poetry vaults into the saddle of the Mediterranean Pegasus and harnesses him to Cuddys and Hobbinols and heighos and roundelays. It is hard, for example, to separate the tang of folksong from the whiff of the classics in 'Come live with me and be my love'. The editors take cognizance of this conventional vision of the period as a takeover move on humanism by the vernacular with a nice discussion of Spenser's 'attempt to find an English Doric' in *The Shepheardes Calendar*, two sections of which are included. Here they note the way the language at one time, in its homely guise, points to an image of recognizable rural reality, and at another, in its 'higher' modes, tends towards masquerade. Such disjunctions are symptomatic of the conflict explored by the anthology as a whole, between pastoral as realistic observation and pastoral as artificial mode.

As the editors point out in the beginning, a similar conflict presents itself in the Eden myth which, together with the classical dream of the Golden Age, lies behind most versions of pastoral. Eden was a garden, an image of harmony between man and nature; it was a place where the owners of the land were the workers of the land, for whom the very land itself worked and produced of its own accord. Yet while the Genesis story gives shape to this persistent dream of paradise (and, by transference, utopia), it also acknowledges the world outside the garden as a place of thorns which man enters in sorrow, to earn his bread by the sweat of his brow. Hence the idealized landscape with contented figures, the garden, the harmonious estate, all the recurring features of the convention, are sanctioned by the race's nostalgia; yet they misrepresent the quotidian actualities of the world man inhabits outside Eden, and in the end beget a form of anti-pastoral in which sweat and pain and deprivation are acknowledged.

Nostalgic dream versus contemporary reality, propertied interests versus the labourer's lot—variations on these themes occur all through the book. Spenser, for example, finally opts for the enamelled world, the dream of an aristocratic English Arcadia, which finds expression in his idealization of Sir Philip Sidney who becomes, in *Astrophel*, 'a gentle shepherd borne in Arcady', and who is represented in Book VI of *The Faerie Queene* first as the chivalrous Sir Calidore and then as Sir Calidore turned shepherd:

> Which Calidore perceiving, thought it best
> To chaunge the manner of his loftie looke;
> And doffing his bright armes himselfe addrest
> In shepheards weed; and in his hand he tooke
> Instead of steele-head speare, a shepheards hooke.

But the editors, in the introductory passage to these Elizabethan poems, have already done some enamel-stripping:

> We can see fairly clearly here the Golden Age being relocated in the myth of the recent feudal past. . . . the first act of the masquerade is followed by a second, as the courtier disguises himself next as a shepherd. The world thus created—in *The Faerie Queene* and in the poems from the *Arcadia*—has far more to do with the dream of an old social order than with that of a prehistoric Golden Age.

This gilding of the age just past is a persistent feature of the poems in the anthology—one thinks immediately of *The Deserted Village*—and it is a strategy by which the disagreeable encroachments of the present are evaded and disagreeable facts in the past elided. When, early in the seventeenth century, Jonson celebrates Penshurst, the house which had been the

176

home of Sir Philip Sidney and so, in a sense, the birthplace of English pastoral, he envisages it as the microcosm of patronage and paternalism. The estate, moreover, is Edenic in its apparently automatic productiveness and harmonious social relationships. But Jonson also acknowledges it as exceptional and, by implicitly indicting the bourgeois individualism of the times, condones the feudal structures of the past and mystifies the economic organization of the present:

> The blushing apricot, and wooly peach
> Hang on thy walls, that every child may reach.
> And though thy walls be of the countrey stone,
> They are rear'd with no mans ruine, no mans grone,
> There's none, that dwell about them, wish them downe;
> But all come in, the farmer and the clowne.

Jonson's poem is echoed bitterly by the last poem in the anthology, Yeats's 'Ancestral Houses', but it also points the way to a more equable and bourgeois mode, where the Virgilian shepherd disappears to have his place taken by the Horatian farmer. The convention of high artificiality at once expires and is apotheosized in the seventeenth century in 'Lycidas', while in Marvell's 'The Garden', the new poetry of retreat mutates naturally out of the old idealized landscape:

> The Garden is a world within the world and not a separation from it; it is a state of individual harmony that has no geographical placement, and is not to be achieved by the labour of men as conventionally understood. The traditional oppositions of pastoral are reconciled in Marvell's 'happy Garden-state', and the Golden Age is relocated in the world of puritan individualism.

While the pastoral idiom and nomenclature reasserted themselves to some cynical purpose after the Restoration, it was the neo-classicism of the eighteenth century that gave the more conventional expressions of the form a new lease of life and in the end inevitably bred the anti-pastoral. The debate, as Pope expressed it in his 'Discourse on Pastoral Poetry', about whether 'we are not to describe our shepherds as shepherds at this day really are, but as they may be conceived then (in the Golden Age) to have been' was actively renewed. Joseph Addison commended the naturalism of Ambrose Philips who had 'given a new life, and a more natural beauty to this way of writing by substituting in the place of these antiquated fables, the superstitious mythology which prevails among the shepherds of our own country', although Philips's Colinets and Cuddys, in their intonation, manner and matter, are still obviously the invention of an urban literary man. There is a more robust and realistic grip on country matters in John Gay's eclogue on 'The Birth of the Squire' which ends with a vision of his death:

> Methinks I see him in his hall appear,
> Where the long table floats in clammy beer,
> 'Midst mugs and glasses shatter'd o'er the floor,
> Dead-drunk his servile crew supinely snore;
> Triumphant, o'er the prostrate brutes he stands,
> The mighty bumper trembles in his hands;
> Boldly he drinks, and like his glorious Sires,
> In copious gulps of potent ale expires.

By 1720, Astrophel was turning in his grave. But some of the most enjoyable, if not exactly deft writing in this Augustan section comes in the attempts at a native georgic, such as John Philips's 'Cyder', more diction than drink:

> Now prepare
> Materials for thy Mill, a study Post
> Cylindric, to support the Grinder's Weight
> Excessive, and a flexile Sallow' entrench'd.
> Rounding, capacious of the juicy Hord.
> Nor must thou not be mindful of thy Press
> Long e'er the Vintage; but with timely Care
> Shave the Goat's shaggy Beard, least thou too late,
> In vain should'st seek a Strainer, to dispart,
> The husky, terrene Dregs, from purer Must.

Two-and-a-half centuries later, this is as unintentionally funny as the squibs by Swift and Richard Jago designed to ridicule a too naïve urban version of the country.

Thomson's 'The Seasons', of course, is central to any consideration of English pastoral verse. It is not a nostalgic poem, because Thomson's Golden Age is contemporary England as after-image of Augustan Rome, a Golden Age characterized not by the absence of labour but by its successful organization. 'The owners of the land that Thomson describes are content to live by the sweat of someone else's brow, if not their own.' But Thomson maintains a crucial synthesis of two attitudes to nature which in the course of the century tend to separate into divergent forms of expression. There is, on the one hand, his sublime celebration of nature's untamed prodigality in the tropics, where paradisal abundance and absence of human cultivation constitute a positive value; on the other hand, there is his commendation of progressive agricultural England, where it is the processes and rewards of labour and the subdued and humanized face of nature that generate the fervent rhetoric. From the first strain of sensibility comes the poetry of the solitary in the unspoiled landscape, a contemplative romantic kind, very different from the Horatian 'happy the man' school: it is represented later in the anthology by extracts from Wordsworth's 'The Excursion', Beattie's 'The Minstrel', Shelley's 'Epipsychidion', and others. From the second there continued the English georgic—Dyer's 'Fleece', Grainger's 'Sugar-Cane' and Christopher Smart's 'Hop Garden', the latter containing such rousing advice to gentlemen-farmers as this specification for a foreman:

> One thing remains unsung, a man of faith
> And long experience, in whose thund'ring voice
> Lives hoarse authority, potent to quell
> The frequent frays of the tumultuous crew.
> He shall preside o'er all thy hopland store,
> Severe dictator!

Still, Stephen Duck's reaction to just such a prop of the economy makes refreshing reading:

> He counts the Bushels, counts how much a Day;
> He swears we've idled half our Time away;
> 'Why look ye, Rogues, d'ye think that this will do?
> 'Your Neighbours thrash as much again as you.'
> Now in our Hands we wish our noisy Tools,
> To drown the hated Names, of Rogues and Fools.
> But wanting these, we just like School-boys look,
> When angry Masters view the blotted Book:
> They cry, 'their Ink was faulty, and their Pen;'
> We, 'the Corn threshes bad, 'twas cut too green'.

With Duck, Crabbe and Clare there emerges the voice that the editors have been waiting to hear, a voice protesting on behalf of the agricultural labourer, who no longer appears as jocund swain or abstract Industry but as a hard-driven human being. It is a voice that has some trouble with its accent—Duck's natural country vigour is soon smoothed out and co-opted by the conventional diction of the period—and it was the unique achievement of John Clare to make vocal the regional and particular, to achieve a buoyant and authentic lyric utterance at the meeting-point between social realism and conventional romanticism. His 'Lament of Swordy Well', printed here, must be one of the best poems of its century.

This anthology is at once an introduction to pastoral and a revisionary reading of it, and I have given little idea of the way it provides a context for the more celebrated examples of the kind. It is a book definitely worth doing and worth having. A sense of the old validity of the pastoral and of its diminution of force in the nineteenth century emerges until one almost agrees with the editors' brisk dismissal of its further possibilities.

Yet I wonder if the story ends as quickly as all that. Obviously, we are unlikely to find new poems about shepherds that will engage us as fully as 'Lycidas', but surely the potent dreaming of a Golden Age or the counter-cultural celebration of simpler life-styles or the nostalgic projection of the garden on childhood are still occasionally continuous with the tradition as it is presented here. If Hopkins's 'Harry Ploughman' gets in, what about Edward Thomas's 'Lob' or Edwin Muir's 'The Horses' or Hugh MacDiarmid's 'Island Funeral'? I can see a case against MacNeice's eclogues, yet they do represent the form as an enabling resource; but is Housman not a definite candidate for inclusion, if only as arch-mystifier? Is the work of David Jones, in pieces like 'The Sleeping Lord', or 'The Tutelar of the Place', not a version of pastoral, based on a visionary nostalgia for an early British Golden Age? It is true that Irish writing was outside the field of reference, but in this area such seminal texts as Synge's *Aran Islands* (prose, granted) and Patrick Kavanagh's *The Great Hunger*, pastoral and anti-pastoral respectively, are not to be regarded just as 'occasional twitches'. And more recently we have had John Montague's *The Rough Field*. Or are these latter works held at bay in the term 'frontier pastoral'?

The Times Literary Supplement, 1975

The God in the Tree

Early Irish Nature Poetry

Early Irish nature poems have been praised and translated often. Their unique cleanliness of line has been commented on. The tang and clarity of a pristine world full of woods and water and birdsong seems to be present in the words. Little jabs of delight in the elemental are communicated by them in a note that is hard to describe. Perhaps Wordsworth's phrase 'surprised by joy' comes near to catching the way some of them combine suddenness and richness—certainly it would do as a title for these eight lines, twenty-two syllables in all, which have etched themselves in the memory of generations, and in English usually go under the title 'The Blackbird of Belfast Lough'.

> The small bird
> let a chirp
> from its beak:
> I heard
> woodnotes, whin-
> gold, sudden.
> The Lagan
> blackbird!

In its precision and suggestiveness, this art has been compared with the art of the Japanese *haiku*. Bashō's frog plopping into its pool in seventeeth-century Japan makes no more durable or exact music than Belfast's blackbird clearing its throat over the lough almost a thousand years earlier.

Equally memorable, compact and concrete are the lines beginning *scel lem duib*, lines that have all the brightness and hardness of a raindrop winking on a thorn. The poem shows us how exactly Flann O'Brien characterized early Irish verse-craft when he spoke about its 'steel-pen exactness', and this is what he

was intent on catching in his version, where the authentic chill
of winter and the bittersweet weather of a northern autumn
pierce into the marrow of the quatrains:

> Here's a song—
> stags give tongue
> winter snows
> summer goes
>
> High cold blow
> sun is low
> brief his day
> seas give spray
>
> Fern clumps redden
> shapes are hidden
> wildgeese raise
> wonted cries.
>
> Cold now girds
> wings of birds
> icy time—
> that's my rhyme.

I can think of only a few poets in English whose words give us
the sharp tooth of winter anywhere as incisively as that: the
medieval poet of *Gawain and the Green Knight* managed it
beautifully, and so did Shakespeare, and Thomas Hardy. That
line in *King Lear*—'still through the sharp hawthorn blows the
cold wind'—has the *frisson* of the bare and shivering flesh about
it, but a touch like that is unusual in English verse. It almost
seems that since the Norman Conquest, the temperature of the
English language has been subtly raised by a warm front coming
up from the Mediterranean. But the Irish language did not
undergo the same Romance influences and indeed early Irish
nature poetry registers certain sensations and makes a
springwater music out of certain feelings in a way unmatched in
any other European language. Kuno Meyer, the pioneering
scholar and translator of Celtic languages, alluded to this distinctive feature when he wrote: 'These poems occupy a unique
position in the literature of the world. To seek out and watch
and love Nature, in its tiniest phenomena as in its grandest, was
given to no people so early and so fully as the Celt.' And

Kenneth Hurlstone Jackson expanded upon that perception in his delightful anthology *A Celtic Miscellany*:

> Comparing these poems with the medieval European lyric is like comparing the emotions of an imaginative adolescent who has just grown to realize the beauty of nature, with those of an old man who has been familiar with it for a lifetime and no longer is able to think of it except in literary terms . . . The truth is that in its earlier period Celtic literature did not belong at all to the common culture of the rest of Europe; nor did it ever become more than partly influenced by it.

On the margin of a ninth-century manuscript, from the monastery of St. Gall in Switzerland, we get another glimpse of nature through the rinsed eyes of Celtic Christianity:

> A wall of forest looms above
>   and sweetly the blackbird sings;
> all the birds make melody
>   over me and my books and things.
>
> There sings to me the cuckoo
>   from bush-citadels in grey hood.
> God's doom! May the Lord protect me
>   writing well, under the great wood.

This poem has been called 'The Scribe in the Woods' and in it we can see the imagination taking its colouring from two very different elements. On the one hand, there is the *pagus*, the pagan wilderness, green, full-throated, unrestrained; on the other hand there is the lined book, the Christian *disciplina*, the sense of a spiritual principle and a religious calling that transcends the almost carnal lushness of nature itself. The writer is as much hermit as scribe, and it is within this anchorite tradition of the early Irish church that early Irish nature poetry develops. Moreover, P. H. Henry in his learned and thrilling study of *The Early English and Celtic Lyric* links this praise poetry with another kind of poem which is its corollary and opposite, a kind we might characterize as penitential poetry. Both spring from a way of life at once simple and ascetic, the tensions of asceticism finding voice in the penitential verse, and the cheerier nature lyrics springing from the solitary's direct experience of the changing seasons.

These two strains are often dramatized vividly in the later

183

Fenian poetry when St. Patrick, the newly arrived missionary
who comes along to disrupt the old heroic order, argues with
Oisin, the unregenerate natural man. Patrick praises the cloister
with its music of massbell and plainsong, Oisin catalogues the
more full-blooded and noisier joys of the hunt or the battle. In
Irish, a whole system of such poems had been elaborated by the
thirteenth century, and continued to develop in subsequent
centuries, when a convention of celebrating specific places also
emerged. This love of place and lamentation against exile from a
cherished territory is another typical strain in the Celtic sensibility, and one poem will here have to represent the whole
extensive genre. I choose Oisin's praise of Ben Bulben, translated by K. H. Jackson from a fifteenth or sixteenth-century
original, partly because it is an early appearance in literature of
the mountain which W. B. Yeats was to impose upon the
imagination of the modern world by his own famous celebration
of its dominant presence in the Sligo landscape. The 'son of
Calpurnius' is, of course, St. Patrick:

> Benn Boilbin that is sad to-day,
> peak that was shapely and best of form,
> at that time, son of Calpurnius,
> it was lovely to be upon its crest.
>
> Many were the dogs and the ghillies,
> the cry of the bugle and the hound,
> and the mighty heroes that were upon your rampart,
> O high peak of the contests.
>
> It was haunted by cranes in the night
> and heath-fowl on its moors,
> with the tuning of small birds
> it was delightful to be listening to them.
>
> The cry of the hounds in its glens,
> the wonderful echo,
> and each of the Fiana
> with lovely dogs on the leash.
>
> Many in the woods were the gleaners
> from the fair women of the Fiana,
> its berries of sweet taste,
> raspberries and blackberries.

184

THE GOD IN THE TREE

Mellow purple blaeberries,
tender cress and cuckoo-flower;
and the curly-haired fair-headed maidens,
sweet was the sound of their singing. . . .

We were on this hill
seven companies of the Fiana;
to-night my friends are few,
and is not my tale pitiful to you.

Scholars might classify this as an elegiac poem as much as a
poem of place and it does indeed have a backward look which
gives it a more modern tone, a more alienated stance; but in the
first flush of the hermit poetry six or seven centuries before this
poem was written, it is not to the tears of things but the joy, the
lifting eye and heart, that we respond. We are nearer the first
world in that first poetry, nearer to the innocent eye and tongue
of Adam as he named the creatures. These next stanzas, for
example, come from a poem put into the mouth of a seventh-
century anchorite from Connacht called Marbhan: even this
literal version conveys the exhilaration of the feeling.

An excellent spring, a cup of noble water to drink; watercresses
sprout, yew berries, ivy bushes as big as a man.

Tame swine lie down around it, goats, boars, wild swine, grazing
deer, a badger's brood . . .

A bush of rowan, black sloes of the dark blackthorn; plenty of food,
acorns, spare berries, pennywort, milk.

A clutch of eggs, honey, produce of wild onions, God has sent it;
sweet apples, red whortleberries, crowberries . . .

A heavy bowlful, goodly hazel nuts, early young corn, brown
acorns, manes of briars, fine sweet tangle . . .

Though you delight in your own enjoyments, greater than all
wealth, for my part I am grateful for what is given me from my dear
Christ.

And so it goes on, the hermit's rhapsody, full of the primeval
energies of the druid's grove. And that word 'druid', of course,
calls up a world older and darker and greener than the world of

185

early Christian Ireland, although some authorities would have it that the role of the *file*, the official poet in historic times, was continuous with the role of the druid in archaic times. I like that possibility a lot because the root of the word 'druid' is related to *doire*, the oak grove, and through that the poet is connected with the mysteries of the grove, and the poetic imagination is linked with the barbaric life of the wood, with Oisin rather than with Patrick.

And this is where I turn to my title, the god in the tree. Poetry of any power is always deeper than its declared meaning. The secret between the words, the binding element, is often a psychic force that is elusive, archaic and only half-apprehended by maker and audience. For example, in the context of monasticism, the god of my title would be the Christian deity, the giver of life, sustainer of nature, creator Father and redeemer Son. But there was another god in the tree, impalpable perhaps but still indigenous, less doctrinally defined than the god of the monasteries but more intuitively apprehended. The powers of the Celtic otherworld hovered there. Ian Finlay, in his *Introduction to Celtic Art*, has noted that it was not until the Romans dominated Gaul and reduced it to a province that the Gaulish or Celtic gods were reduced to the likenesses of living men and women; before that, the deities remained shrouded in the living matrices of stones and trees, immanent in the natural world. Indeed, when we think of all the taboos and awe surrounding the fairy thorn in the Irish countryside until very recently, and of the pilgrimages which still go on in places to the ancient holy wells, there is no problem about acknowledging the reality of Finlay's statements. So I want to suggest that this early poetry is sustained by a deep unconscious affiliation to the old mysteries of the grove, even while ardently proclaiming its fidelity to the new religion. After all, there is no reason why literature should not bear these traces as well as the architecture: the old religion kept budding out on the roofs of cathedrals all over Europe, in the shape of those roof-bosses which art historians call 'green men' or 'foliate heads', human faces growing out of and into leaves and acorns and branches.

And those green men remind me of another foliate head, another wood-lover and tree-hugger, a picker of herbs and drinker from wells: I am thinking, of course, of Mad Sweeney, who is the hero of a sequence of poems that bears his name, and who was at once the enemy and the captive of the monastic tradition. In the story, Sweeney is a petty king who is cursed by St. Ronan to be turned into a bird and live a life of expiation exposed to the hardships and delights of the seasons until, at the end, he is retrieved for the church by St. Moling who records his history and his poems. One of these poems is clearly very old, continuous with archaic lore, but rendered literary and dainty by long familiarity. This is Sweeney's praise of the trees themselves, another paean to nature's abundance, another thanksgiving, another testimony to the nimbus of the woods in the Celtic imagination.

> The bushy leafy oaktree
> is highest in the wood,
> the forking shooting hazel
> has nests of hazel-nut.
>
> The alder is my darling,
> all thornless in the gap,
> some milk of human kindness
> coursing in its sap.
>
> The blackthorn is a jaggy creel
> stippled with dark sloes,
> green watercress is thatch on wells
> where the drinking blackbird goes.
>
> Sweetest of the leafy stalks,
> the vetches strew the pathway,
> the oyster-grass is my delight
> and the wild strawberry.
>
> Ever-generous apple-trees
> rain big showers when shaken;
> scarlet berries clot like blood
> on mountain rowan.
>
> Briars curl in sideways,
> arch a stickle back,
> draw blood, and curl up innocent
> to sneak the next attack.

The yew tree in each churchyard
wraps night in its dark hood.
Ivy is a shadowy
genius of the wood.

Holly rears its windbreak,
a door in winter's face;
life-blood on a spear-shaft
darkens the grain of ash.

Birch tree, smooth and blessed,
delicious to the breeze,
high twigs plait and crown it
the queen of trees.

The aspen pales
and whispers, hesitates:
a thousand frightened scuts
race in its leaves.

But what disturbs me
more than anything
is an oak rod, always
testing its thong.

That is only one of Sweeney's innumerable outbursts where his imagination is beautifully entangled with the vegetation and the weathers and animals of the countryside, and it will have to stand for scores of similar poems from the sixth to the sixteenth century, all of them attesting to the god in the tree as a source of poetic inspiration.

I have not given an inclusive catalogue of the poems. Anybody interested will find much help and pleasure in the works of Robin Flower, Kuno Meyer, K. H. Jackson, Gerard Murphy, Frank O'Connor and David Greene, James Carney; in anthologies of Irish verse by John Montague and Brendan Kennelly; and in surveys of the Celtic world by writers such as Nora Chadwick, Myles Dillon and Alwyn Rhys. I have confined myself to poems that have had an enhancing effect on my own imagination and have simply tried to account for the peculiar nature of that effect. And I want to end with a moment which, I feel, is relevant to all that I have been considering, a moment that was a kind of small epiphany. This was eleven years ago, at Gallarus Oratory, on the Dingle Peninsula, in Co. Kerry, an early Christian, dry-stone oratory, about the size of a large turf-stack. Inside, in the dark of the stone, it feels as if you are sustaining a great pressure, bowing under like the generations of monks who must have bowed down in meditation and reparation on that floor. I felt the weight of Christianity in all its rebuking aspects, its calls to self-denial and self-abnegation, its humbling of the proud flesh and insolent spirit. But coming out of the cold heart of the stone, into the sunlight and the dazzle of grass and sea, I felt a lift in my heart, a surge towards happiness that must have been experienced over and over again by those monks as they crossed that same threshold centuries ago. This surge towards praise, this sudden apprehension of the world as light, as illumination, this is what remains central to our first nature poetry and makes it a unique inheritance.

Radio Telefís Eireann, 1978

Canticles to the Earth

*Theodore Roethke**

A couple of years ago, an American poet told me that he and his generation had rejected irony and artfulness, and were trying to write poems that would not yield much to the investigations of the practical criticism seminar. And another poet present agreed, yes, he was now looking at English poetry to decide which areas seemed most in need of renovation, and then he was going to provide experiments that would enliven these sluggish, provincial backwaters. As poets, both seemed to be infected with wrong habits of mind. They had imbibed attitudes into their writing life which properly belong to the lecturer and the anthologist: a concern with generations, with shifting fashions of style, a belief that their role was complementary and responsible to a demonstrable literary situation. For although at least one spirit of the age will probably be discernible in a poet's work, he should not turn his brain into a butterfly net in pursuit of it.

An awareness of his own poetic process, and a trust in the possibility of his poetry, that is what a poet should attempt to preserve; and whatever else Theodore Roethke may have lacked, he did possess and nourish this faith in his own creative instincts. His current flies continuously:

> Water's my will and my way,
> And the spirit runs, intermittently,
> In and out of the small waves,
> Runs with the intrepid shorebirds—
> How graceful the small before danger!

* Theodore Roethke, *Collected Poems*, Faber, 1968.

But the most remarkable thing about this watery spirit of his is that for all its motion, it never altogether finds its final bed and course. Through one half of the work, it is contained in the strict locks of rhyme and stanzaic form; through the other, it rises and recedes in open forms like floods in broad meadows.

His first book has the quiet life of an old canal. 'Vernal Sentiment' would not be an unjust title for the volume. All the conflicting elements in Roethke's make-up are toned down and contained in well-behaved couplets and quatrains. The sense of fun is coy, the sense of natural forces explicit and the sense of form a bit monotonous. It is partly a case of the young man putting a hand across his daimon's mouth, for although the first poem calls:

> My secrets cry aloud.
> I have no need for tongue.
> My heart keeps open house,
> My doors are widely swung

we have to read the whole book to believe it. Indeed the life's work is neatly bracketed by the first and last lines of this collected volume. We move from 'My secrets cry aloud' to 'With that he hitched his pants and humped away,' and between the rhetoric and the rumbustiousness the true achievement is located.

That achievement arrives from the boundaries of Roethke's experience: childhood and death are elements in which his best work lives. And love. He grew up in Michigan among his father's extensive greenhouses: 'They were to me, I realize now, both heaven and hell, a kind of tropics created in the savage climate of Michigan, where austere German-Americans turned their love of order and their terrifying efficiency into something truly beautiful. It was a universe, several worlds, which, even as a child, one worried about and struggled to keep alive.'

Growth, minute and multifarious life, became Roethke's theme. His second collection, *The Lost Son*, contained the famous greenhouse poems, a repossession of the childhood Eden. Now the free, nervous notation of natural process issues in a sense of unity with cosmic energies and in quiet intimations

191

of order and delight. They are acts of faith made in some state of grace:

> I can hear, underground, that sucking and sobbing,
> In my veins, in my bones I feel it,—
> The small waters seeping upward,
> The tight grains parting at last.
> When sprouts break out,
> Slippery as fish,
> I quail, lean to beginnings, sheath-wet.

Such celebration, however, was prelude to disturbance and desperation. Out of Eden man takes his way, and beyond the garden life is riotous; chaos replaces correspondence, consciousness thwarts communion, the light of the world fades in the shadow of death. Until the final serenity and acceptance of all things in a dance of flux, which comes in the posthumous *The Far Field*, Roethke's work is driven in two opposite directions by his fall into manhood.

In the final poems of *The Lost Son* volume and in all the work of *Praise to the End* there is an apocalyptic straining towards unity. These are large, sectioned poems, ghosted by the rhythms of nursery rhyme. You feel that the archetypal properties are being manipulated a bit arbitrarily, that the staccato syntax is for effect rather than effective and that in general the sense of fractured relations between the man and his physical and metaphysical elements is deliberately shrouded. These poems are more like constructs for the inarticulate than raids upon it. Yet despite the occasional echo of Dylan Thomas, they retain the authentic Roethke note, the note of energy and quest:

> Everything's closer. Is this a cage?
> The chill's gone from the moon.
> Only the woods are alive.
> I can't marry the dirt.

In direct contrast to these wandering tides of the spirit, there follows a series of tightly controlled and elaborately argued meditations and love poems. After the fidgety metres and the surrealism, he begins to contain his impulses to affirmation in a rapid, iambic line which owes much to Raleigh and Sir John Davies, even though in a moment of exuberance he declares:

I take this cadence from a man named Yeats,
I take it, and I give it back again.

The poems tend to have a strict shape and lively rhythm ('the shapes a bright container can contain!') and deal with the possibility of momentary order, harmony and illumination. Love and lyric are modes of staying the confusion and fencing off emptiness. Within the glass walls of the poem, something of the old paradisal harmony can be feigned:

> Dream of a woman, and a dream of death:
> The light air takes my being's breath away;
> I look on white, and it turns into gray—
> When will that creature give me back my breath?
> I live near the abyss. I hope to stay
> Until my eyes look at a brighter sun
> As the thick shade of the long night comes on.

There is a curious split in Roethke's work between the long Whitmanesque cataloguing poem, which works towards resolution by accumulating significant and related phenomena, and this other brisk, traditional artefact that dances to its own familiar music. Perhaps the explanation lies in Roethke's constant natural urge to praise, to maintain or recapture ecstasy.

The more relaxed and loaded form includes his best poems, all of which exhale something of a Franciscan love of every living thing, and invoke the notion of a divine unity working through them. They are canticles to the earth, if you like, written in a line that has exchanged its 'barbaric yawp' for a more civil note of benediction. On the other hand, when he is not in full possession of his emotion, when tranquillity is missing, then he employs the artificer's resources of metre, stanza and rhyme to conduct himself and the poem towards a provisional statement. The stanzaic poems always sound as if they are attempting something. The best Roethke, the praise poetry, always gives the impression that the lines came ripe and easy as windfalls.

Ripeness is all in the latest work, which appeared in this country two years after his death. In one of the poems he mentions 'that sweet man, John Clare', and one is reminded how both poets lived near the abyss but resolved extreme experience into something infinitely gentle. In the light of their last days, 'all's a scattering, a shining'. Their suffering breeds something larger than masochism. Roethke reflects when his field-mouse departs for the hazard of the fields:

I think of the nestling fallen into the deep grass,
The turtle gasping in the dusty rubble of the highway,
The paralytic stunned in the tub, and the water rising,—
All things innocent, hapless, forsaken.

He is outside movements and generations, and his work is a true growth. He seems destined to grudging notice because he echoed the voices of other poets, or because people have grown afraid of the gentle note that was his own, but the *Collected Poems* are there, a true poet's testament:

Pain wanders through my bones like a lost fire;
What burns me now? Desire, desire, desire.

Listener, 1968

Tradition and an Individual Talent

*Hugh MacDiarmid**

Though he would have been the last to admit any comparison of himself with an Englishman, Hugh MacDiarmid's poetic career reminds me of Wordsworth's. Both discovered early a way of affiliating an individual talent to a submerged tradition; both professed a diction that was deliberately at variance with prevalent modes; both wrote classic lyric poetry in a short period of intense creativity and followed this by turning their lyric discoveries towards more ambitious goals, producing long meditative poems that wove their personal poetic and public worlds into a single major artistic form. *The Prelude* and *A Drunk Man Looks at the Thistle* are the central achievements in the Wordsworth and MacDiarmid canons, emerging as plateaus of typical excellence towards which the earlier work was leading and in the shadow of which their later work is inevitably viewed.

Again like the young Wordsworth, MacDiarmid has a sense of an enervating cultural situation—he saw Scottish civilization as damned and doomed by influences from south of the Border—that is intimately linked with his linguistic obsessions. He set out not so much to purify as to restore the language of the tribe, with a passion that was as philological as it was poetic. Dictionaries are necessary to his diction. Lallans, his poetic Scots language, is based on the language of men, specifically on the dialect of his home district around Langholm in Dumfriesshire, but its attractive gaudiness is qualified by the not infrequent inanities of his English, for he occasionally speaks a language that the ones in Langholm do not know. You get on

* Michael Grieve and Alexander Scott, *The Hugh MacDiarmid Anthology*, Routledge and Kegan Paul, 1972.

the one hand the self-delighting flood of 'Water Music' where the Scots and the latinate English furl together in a downpour of energy:

> Archin' here and arrachin there,
>   Allevolie or allemand,
> Whiles appliable, whiles areird,
>   The polysemous poem's planned.
> Lively, louch, atweesh, atween,
>   Auchimuty or aspate,
> Threidin' through the averins,
>   Or bightsom in the aftergait.

Here is a poetry that communicates before it is understood, where the auditory imagination is entirely capable of penetrating to a basic meaning spoken by the music of the vocabulary, alien though that vocabulary may be. On the other hand, how are you to respond to this, from 'On a Raised Beach'?

> What artist poses the Earth écorché thus,
> Pillar of creation engouled me?
> What eburnation augments you with men's bones,
> Every energumen an Endymion yet?
> All the other stones are in this haeccity it seems.
> But where is the Christophanic rock that moved?
> What Cabirian song from this catasta comes?

There is an uncertainty about language here, peculiar not just to MacDiarmid, but to others who write generally in English, but particularly out of a region where the culture and language are at variance with standard English utterance and attitudes.

It can be a problem of style for Americans, West Indians, Indians, Scots and Irish. Joyce made a myth and a mode out of this self-consciousness, but he did so by taking on the English language itself and wrestling its genius with his bare hands, making it lie down where all its ladders start, in the rag-and-bone shop of Indo-European origins and relationships. And it is this Joyce of *Finnegans Wake* who is invoked in the introductory verse of 'Water Music':

> Wheest, wheesht, Joyce, and let me hear
>   Nae Anna Livvy's lilt,
> But Wauchope, Esk and Ewes again
>   Each wi' its ain rhythms till't.

In the poem, the local and the indigenous, which were Joyce's obsession also, are affiliated to oral and instinctive characteristics of the region and the intensity and volubility of the regional diction, while they embody both personal feeling and technical virtuosity, eschew experiment and cosmopolitan perspectives, indulge in no comparative or all-inclusive mythology of rivers. The man who writes the poem is manifestly literate but opts for a local geography and idiom that aspires to subdue rather than include the world in its little room.

'On a Raised Beach' proceeds on completely different lines. If Burns and Dunbar are tributaries in the stream of Lallans, the portentous and absurd shadow of William McGonagall sometimes haunts MacDiarmid's English. The epic voice goes epileptic:

> Diallage of the world's debate, end of the long auxesis,
> Although no ebrillade of Pegasus can here avail,
> I prefer your enchorial characters—the futhore of the future—
> To the hieroglyphics of all other forms of Nature.

In attempting a poetry of ideas MacDiarmid can write like a lunatic lexicographer. What is missing in his phantasmagoric English is what Joyce possessed in such abundance, the sense of the ridiculous, a compulsion to parody. When his brow furrows with earnest ambition and his pedantic Scottish pipe begins its relentless drone we witness the amazing metamorphosis of genius into bore. He decks out the insights of a poet with the egregious jargons of the encyclopaedia and while his intention is explicit in 'The Kind of Poetry I Want'—'a poetry full of erudition, expertise and ecstasy', 'a poetry like an operating theatre', a marxist-humanist poetry of modern consciousness and experience—his execution is often such as to bring his great gifts to the level of bathos. Yet when he succeeds, as he does with a fluency and dignity in 'Island Funeral', the result is an unusually direct and central seriousness, a man speaking to men.

In *A Drunk Man Looks at the Thistle*, MacDiarmid retrieves for modern poetry the image of the poet offered by the Preface to the *Lyrical Ballads*: a man endued with a lively sensibility, unusual enthusiasm and tenderness, a great knowledge of human nature, a comprehensive soul, a man rejoicing in the spirit of life that is in him and delighted to contemplate similar volitions and passions as manifested in the goings-on of the universe. The poem is written in Scots and has for its protagonist a man full of Scotch whisky—even that has been adulterated, 'the stuffie's no' the real Mackay'—playing truant in a ditch from a wife that he loves, through one whole moonlit night. Such a persona in such a situation allows MacDiarmid to dramatize an amazing number of moods, express opinions, achieve 'pure' and 'didactic' effects, be comic, elegaic, satiric or tragic as the drink burns or dies in the speaker. He is more full-bodied than Tiresias, more domesticated than Crazy Jane, more raucous than Crispin, but despite his local accent, he speaks on equal terms with these memorable creations of our time.

Hibernia, 1972

A Memorable Voice

Stevie Smith*

Always inclined to the brisk definition, W. H. Auden once declared that poetry was memorable speech. The *Collected Poems* of the late Stevie Smith prompt one to revise that: poetry is memorable voice. The unknown quantity in my response to the book was the memory of the poet's own performance of her verse, her voice pitching between querulousness and keening, her quizzical presence at once inviting the audience to yield her their affection and keeping them at bay with a quick irony. She seemed to combine elements of Gretel and of the witch, to be vulnerable and capable, a kind of Home Counties *sean bhean bhocht*, with a hag's wisdom and a girl's wide-eyed curiosity. She chanted her poems artfully off-key, in a beautifully flawed plainsong that suggested two kinds of auditory experience: an embarrassed party-piece by a child half-way between tears and giggles, and a deliberate *faux-naif* rendition by a virtuoso.

This raises the whole question of poetry for the eye versus poetry for the ear. Perhaps the *versus* is an overstatement, yet there are poets whose work is enhanced and amplified in its power to move once we know the characteristic tone and rhythm and texture of the poet's physical voice. The grave inward melodies of Wallace Stevens become more available if we happen to have heard that Caedmon recording of him reading 'The Idea of Order at Key West'. Similarly, Robert Frost's words are enlivened by any memory of his switchback pacing, the hard and fluent contours of his accent. And I am sure that Coleridge's excitement on first hearing Wordsworth read was as much a matter of how the poem sounded as of what it intended.

* Stevie Smith, *Collected Poems*, Allen Lane, 1975.

But in the case of Stevie Smith, it is not simply a matter of extra gratification from the poems on the page if we happen to have heard her. It is the whole question of the relationship between a speaking voice, a literary voice (or style) and a style of speech shared by and typical of a certain social and cultural grouping. In other words, it is essential to bring to the appreciation of these poems an ear aware of the longueurs and acerbities, the nuanced understatements and tactical intonations of educated middle-class English speech. The element this work survives in is a disenchanted gentility, and while I can imagine, for example, the Reverend Ian Paisley making a fine job of Yeats's 'Under Ben Bulben', I cannot imagine Stevie Smith's idiosyncratic rhythms and metres surviving the hammer-and-tongue of that vigorous North Antrim emphasis.

One is tempted to use words like 'fey', 'arch' and 'dotty' when faced with these five hundred and seventy pages and yet such adjectives sell Stevie Smith's work short. These odd syncopated melancholy poems are haunted by the primitive and compelling music of ballad and nursery rhyme, but it has been transposed by a sophisticated and slightly cosseted poetic ear into a still, sad, drawing-room music of humanity:

> He said no word of her to us
> Nor we of her to him,
> But oh it saddened us to see
> How wan he grew and thin.
> We said: She eats him day and night
> And draws the blood from him,
> We did not know but said we thought
> This was why he grew thin.

There is variety and inventiveness, much humour and understanding, and a constant poignancy. Her gift was to create a peculiar emotional weather between the words, a sense of pity for what is infringed and unfulfilled, as in the much anthologized 'Not Waving but Drowning', or in this one, taken almost at random:

> I always remember your beautiful flowers
> And the beautiful kimono you wore
> When you sat on the couch
> With that tigerish crouch
> And told me you loved me no more.

200

What I cannot remember is how I felt when you were unkind
All I know is, if you were unkind now I should not mind.
Ah me, the power to feel exaggerated, angry and sad
The years have taken from me,
    Softly I go now, pad pad.

Stevie Smith reminds you of two Lears: the old king come to knowledge and gentleness through suffering, and the old comic poet Edward veering off into nonsense. I suppose in the end the adjective has to be 'eccentric'. She looks at the world with a mental squint, there is a disconcerting wobble in the mirror she holds up to nature.

Death, waste, loneliness, cruelty, the maimed, the stupid, the innocent, the trusting—her concerns were central ones, her compassion genuine and her vision almost tragic. Yet finally the voice, the style, the literary resources are not adequate to the sombre recognitions, the wounded *joie de vivre*, the marooned spirit we sense they were destined to express. There is a retreat from resonance, as if the spirit of A. A. Milne successfully vied with the spirit of Emily Dickinson.

The genetic relations which the forms of these poems often bear to the clerihew and the caricature prevent them from attaining the kind of large orchestration that they are always tempting us to listen for. And if they are the real thing when measured by Auden's definition, they miss the absolute intensity required by Emily Dickinson's definition: when you read them, you don't feel that the top of your head has been taken off. Rather, you have been persuaded to keep your head at all costs.

Irish Times, 1976

The Labourer and the Lord

*Francis Ledwidge and Lord Dunsany**

Francis Ledwidge and Lord Dunsany were both Meath men, much favoured in their birthplace, minor writers who had glimpses of the shaping of Ireland's future when the mists on the Bog of Allen were occasionally troubled by rhetoric or explosions from Dublin or Westminster or Flanders. Ledwidge's muse was the hearth-guardian of a labourer's cottage, Dunsany's a Gothic beldame in the corridors of Dunsany Castle. A relationship developed between the cottage and the castle, the ganger of the roadworks team playing grateful poet to the noble lord's undoubtedly generous patronage. While their surviving letters are by no means classics, they do indicate a genuine exchange and nurture in the relationship, hampered by Ledwidge's modesty and self-taught literariness and Dunsany's breezy complacency.

Ledwidge was killed in France in 1918, having survived two fronts in Gallipoli and Salonica, and a deep wound in his emotions when the Easter Rising occurred in his absence. His photograph has the tragic melancholy of all those doomed soldiers: but behind it was an unusually sensitive, tenacious and tormented nature. Brought up in poverty by a widowed mother who was the first to give him a sense of kinship with the feminine slopes and levels of the Boyne valley, he was in turn farmer's boy, roadman, ganger, insurance clerk and soldier. He was nicknamed 'The Blackbird' by his friends in the country, but he emerges from the pages of Alice Curtayne's serene and

* Alice Curtayne, *Francis Ledwidge*, Martin Brian and O'Keefe, 1972; Mark Amory, *Lord Dunsany*, Lord Dunsany, *My Talks with Dean Spanley* and *The Curse of the Wise Woman*, Collins, 1972.

faithful biography as a worried cyclist, pedalling at dusk to genteel trysts with rich farmers' daughters, or setting off on a bad morning for the works or the office. Miss Curtayne has an exact sense of the texture of that rural world where he came to consciousness, and is at her best in conveying the impact of political movements and public events on the hungry sensibility of a bachelor labourer living in Slane during the first two decades of the century.

His tensions might be represented in his sporting interests—he played Gaelic football for the local team but liked to be in on the cricket which Dunsany arranged each summer; or in his literary affiliations—he was friendly with Thomas MacDonagh, executed in 1916, and wrote his best-known poem to his memory, yet his first volume was introduced to the world by a Unionist peer and published while he was serving with the British Army.

He was actively involved in the labour movement and a passionate supporter of the Irish Volunteers who broke from the National Volunteers when John Redmond virtually turned the latter into a recruiting ground for the British Army. Yet despite his manifest Sinn Fein sympathies, Ledwidge himself eventually joined up. Miss Curtayne clears Dunsany of the blame which nationalist opinion has laid on him for coaxing the poet into the ranks, and convincingly outlines the distressing process of the decision, imagining it to happen, typically, on a bicycle. Her book is informed by a nice compassion, sensible of the pieties and strains at work in Ledwidge's imagination, and written with a slight pastoral tinge entirely appropriate to its subject. She is no literary critic, but one is grateful for her attentive, unspectacular enterprise in setting down the tale which, including as it does the talk and letters of Ledwidge's surviving acquaintances, is his right, authentic elegy.

Both Ledwidge and Dunsany dreamt of fame. For Ledwidge it was the possible reward for service and labour in an art; for Dunsany it was a damned irritating quarry that seemed to rise for other chaps though never for him, but, by Gad, he gave it a run for its money. An early introduction to the conspiring realms of the Celtic Twilight seemed to promise recognition and association with great names. He had plays performed at the Abbey and in London, published stories of gods and magical heroes, entertained Yeats, Lady Gregory, AE and Gogarty (his wife's diary is excellent on this), met actors and publishers, and began a collaboration with Sidney Sime, the popular illustrator. Yet he ended up congratulating himself that photographers and autograph-hunters sought him out on the American lecture circuit.

The writing appears as a strange manic eddy in the current of his life: 'A rough time-table evolved in the years after his marriage: winter and shooting at Dunsany, May and June at first in London, later in Kent, back to Dunsany for summer and cricket, September in Yorkshire always for partridges at Arden Hall with Lord and Lady Mexborough, then Scotland for grouse, before October and November in London.' If an actor or producer came to Dunsany Castle, he might dash off a play in the afternoon and hand it over, like an enthusiastic schoolboy, at dinner-time. But while his star seemed to be rising, the intellect of this man saw no need to choose between perfection of the life or of the work. In 1916 he wrote that 'genius is in fact an infinite capacity for not taking pains'; in 1934, 'the more the intellect is used, the less in my opinion is the man an artist.' On which his biographer comments with indulgent irony that Dunsany had an intellect but did not use it in his work, his politics, or indeed at all, except when playing chess.

Mr. Amory is far too indulgent. He does not 'read' his man, but records his busy life as the subject might have viewed it himself. It is one way, I suppose, yet I kept waiting for a point of view, a style, an acerbity, something that would place Dunsany's attitudes and antics. The peer was an extraordinary man, the Tory landlord ('he had 1,400 acres at Dunsany but no interest in farming') and the fantasist (author of *The Gods of Pegana*, *The King of Elfland's Daughter*, typical titles among the fifty or so to his name, including, in 1934, *If I were Dictator*!)—both spirits inhabiting the same barbarian frame. There was some quarrel with himself which Mr. Amory might have brought into focus, but, as it is, Dunsany emerges as a character who might be played to perfection by Terry-Thomas in *Carry on, M'Lud*.

His capacity for self-aggrandizement was immense, his inclination to self-scrutiny nil. There was charm (Kipling was fond of him), kindness (he managed Ledwidge's publications and helped him with money) and boorishness: an overbearing sense of himself as the cynosure of neighbouring eyes. Even when there were no eyes to see, he behaved dramatically.

> He wrote in pencil, coloured crayon or if in ink, with quills, often plucked from geese he had shot himself. Swan quills were even bigger and better, but not so easy to get. For an hour or two all was tense. No one must whistle. The saw-mill ceased.

He once sacked a servant who unlocked the gate to a neighbour during his séance. Certainly what we get from Mr. Amory is nearly the whole story, but there is a better, tarter book immanent in this uncritical record.

Dunsany's *Talks with Dean Spanley*, as Mr. Amory observes, has two jokes, 'that the Dean can half-remember his former incarnation as a dog and that it is necessary to get him rather drunk before he can, or will, do so; but they are well-sustained.' I think they are not. Dunsany was not the man to divide this stale loaf and fish even among a hundred pages of rather large print. It is vacuous whimsy for dog-lovers and those amused by what its protagonist would no doubt describe as 'sly humour'.

The other reissue, *The Curse of the Wise Woman*, is much more interesting. Its hero is abroad, engaged on some diplomatic business for the new Irish Free State, and the book is a nostalgic evocation of an adolescence during the Troubles. The emotional division in the heart of a Unionist landlord, living in a newly independent Ireland, is emblematically realized in the setting. The boy hovers between the privileged structures of Eton and his walled estate, and the mysterious lure of the bog and its denizens. The hero's world is masculine and feudal, its spirit is the gun and dog; the primeval landscape beyond the walls is feminine, its spirit is the wise woman. Both are threatened by the impersonal enterprise of the Peat Development (Ireland) Syndicate. While the characters are two-dimensional and some of the dialogue a parody of stage Irish, these are the constituents of what might be a myth for the shaping of modern Ireland, and while the author balks it with a happy ending that is imaginatively unsatisfactory and geologically improbable (a tidal wave of bog engulfs the machines), the book contains many exhilarating sportsman's sketches, and there is a seam of memorable beauty running through the whole story, in the evocations of the mythopoeic bog. It is a pity Dunsany didn't spend more time and intellect exploring these peaty obsessions.

Listener, 1972

The Poetry of John Hewitt*

John Hewitt's career proceeds quietly and steadily through movements and fashions at its own pace, 'a walking pace', to use his own description. Auden, Dylan Thomas, Larkin and Hughes have all left their traces on the decades they dominated, but Hewitt's voice matures and relaxes within its own discipline.

The demands of that discipline are implied in his reviews: an emphasis on the poet as maker, a concern for professional standards in the handling of form, a distrust of freedom and extravagance that has not been earned by toil within the traditional modes. Of Padraic Colum he wrote:

> He is no artless bard, merely instinctive in his song. He knows what he is doing, and from now on will, for me, be the greater man for that.

Of Austin Clarke:

> Clarke, who so often before in his verse-making was as impersonal as a medieval enameller whose care was not for himself but for the chalice and the intricate perfection of his art, now speaks out in his proper person—

and one feels the unspoken comment that it is only after such an immersion in the craft that the personal statement will have poetic validity. A few short phrases will suffice to fill out the picture—'Irish poets, learn your trade'; 'technically, he is too careless'; 'awkwardness not merely risked but fully achieved'; 'insecure metrics, commonplace diction'. And finally a reminder to myself: 'I give no weight or authority to any review of poetry that fights shy of quotation.'

* John Hewitt, *Collected Poems 1932–67*, MacGibbon and Kee, 1968.

207

Quotation will suffice to show Hewitt's own tense care in the
handling of metre, rhyme and stanza:

> Tho' many things I love should disappear
> in the black night ahead of us, I know
> I shall remember, silent, crouching there,
> your pale face gazing where the rushes grow,
> seeking between the tall stems for the last
> black chick the grebe is cruising round to find,
> my pointing finger showing it not lost
> but sheltered only from the ruffling wind.

This has an almost Augustan poise and directness, married to
an elegiac, inward note, and inhabits a typical Hewitt area,
halfway between statement and evocation. For although he
refers to his 'strong opinions, vanities', the verse itself rarely
raises its voice, relying on tone, understatement and oblique
reference to make its more astringent points.

For example, the matter of cultural, historical and religious divisions in the North of Ireland enters the poetry at a
personal or dramatic level, never as opinion. A number of these
poems reveal a quest for personal identity that must strike many
of Hewitt's fellow-countrymen as a remembrance, full of a
stubborn determination to belong to the Irishry and yet tenaci-
ously aware of a different origin and cast of mind. A dramatic
monologue converts the Ulster planter's experience into a
Roman situation where the citizens of the colony are on the
verge of turning native:

> The use, the pace, the patient years of labour,
> the rain against the lips, the changing light,
> the heavy clay-sucked stride, have altered us;
> we would be strangers in the Capitol;
> this is our country also, no-where else;
> and we shall not be outcast on the world.

And this is complemented by the poet's personal nostalgia for a
language, completely possessed. Just as Stephen Dedalus
envied the English Jesuit his total inheritance of the English
language, Hewitt longs for a fullness of speech:

> well rubbed words that had left their overtones
> in the ripe England of the moulded downs

208

and he declares himself ill at ease yet envious also in the presence of the country people whom he embraced for a community of spirit:

> I've tried to learn the smaller parts of speech
> in your slow language, but my thoughts need more
> flexible shapes to move in.

Perhaps this two-way pull, back into the grave and eloquent mainstream of English and out into the shifting, elaborate, receding currents of the Irish experience, lies behind Hewitt's poetic voice, a voice that inclines to plainness but yields to the drift and suggestion of a rhythm, that begins to declare but evolves towards introspection, that seeks 'thought' (a favourite word) but occupies itself much of the time with the rough edges of the actual.

Roughly, the pattern shows an early period when he examines himself against his native community; then, after his shift to England in 1957, he sets his lonely present against a rooted past, in terms of a lost community and family; and finally, his sensibility surrenders to an inundation by the far but half-remembered world of Greece. This is an accumulation of honesty and craft, with its beautiful pointed moments of definition and its inevitable realizations of development. The first poem in the collection, 'Ireland', opens a vein that is worked for years:

> We are not native here or anywhere.
> We were the keltic wave that broke over Europe,
> and ran up this bleak beach among these stones:
> but when the tide ebbed, were left stranded here
> in crevices and ledge-protected pools.

Then his shedding of an Ulster past is lodged in the metaphor of 'Jacob and the Angel':

> I will not pause to struggle with my past,
> locked in an angry posture with a ghost,
> but, striding forward, trust the sunken thigh.

Later still, in 'The Modelled Head', an extremely moving poem of self-examination and revelation, the determination not to let attitudes harden into postures is teased from the poet's consideration of his own sculptured head—

> and I am left with these alternatives,
> to find a new mask for what I wish to be,
> or try to be a man without a mask,
> resolved not to grow neutral, growing old.

Perhaps John Hewitt's attention to the craft of poetry in his earlier period, his devotion to the couplet, the sonnet, the blank verse, the intense and muted lyric, could be regarded as a mask for what he wished to be—faithful to a heritage, rooted within a tradition.

Shouldered out of his island on to 'The Mainland' and knowing that if he sails back he will 'find it rich in all but what he sought', he is evolving into a man without a mask. The verse has become free, the statements grope towards something irreducible:

> Hand over hand eagerly I crawl
> back to uncertainty.

That is the kind of authority without dogma that poets stand for and John Hewitt's collection will be cherished for what has been familiar to us—poems like 'The Owl' and 'Hedgehog'—and for those other accurate, painful quests towards self-knowledge that at once rebuke and reward us.

Threshold, 1972

The Mixed Marriage

*Paul Muldoon**

Paul Muldoon's first book was aptly titled *New Weather*: it introduced us to a distinctive sensibility, a supple inward music, a poetry that insisted on its proper life as words before it conceded the claims of that other life we all live before and after words. *Mules* continues and develops this hermetic direction and is a strange, rich second collection, reminding one sometimes of the sophisticated repose of *poésie pure*, and sometimes bringing one down to earth in the simple piety of the local ballad. It is as if the poems spring from some mixed imaginative marriage, as if their genesis is mule-like, and indeed one excellent entry-point into the book is a poem called 'The Mixed Marriage'. I quote it in full, because I feel that with this poet it is essential to hear the delicate tone, half-way between cajolement and disdain, and the deft transitions, half-way between the playful and the poignant:

> My father was a servant-boy.
> When he left school at eight or nine
> He took up billhook and loy
> To win the ground he would never own.
>
> My mother was the school-mistress,
> The world of Castor and Pollux.
> There were twins in her own class.
> She could never tell which was which.
>
> She had read one volume of Proust,
> He knew the cure for farcy.
> I flitted between a hole in the hedge
> And a room in the Latin Quarter.

*Paul Muldoon, *Mules*, Faber, 1977.

When she had cleared the supper-table
She opened The Acts of the Apostles,
Aesop's Fables, Gulliver's Travels.
Then my mother went on upstairs

And my father further dimmed the light
To get back to hunting with ferrets
Or the factions of the faction-fights,
The Ribbon Boys, the Caravats.

Of course, the first thing there is the melody, the play on the octosyllabic metronome, a music that by its deliberation and technical self-assurance belies the naif wording. There is a connoisseur's savouring of the dialect and of the arcane in farcy, Caravats, billhook and loy, ferrets and faction-fights, all of which invite us to indulge a version of Ulster pastoral. But that indulgence is just disallowed by Proust and the Latin Quarter, not to mention Castor and Pollux and *Gulliver's Travels*. It is as if the imagination is fathered by the local subculture on the mothering literate culture of the schools. Muldoon's is a sceptical, playful imagination, capable of allegory and parable, in poems like 'How to Play Championship Tennis' and 'At Martha's Deli', in love with riddles and hints and half-disclosures in poems like 'Cheesecake', 'Boon', 'The Country Club' and 'Duffy's Circus', but finally at its richest when it dwells and broods over one suggestive image—'The Merman', for example—until that image slowly and richly begins a series of metamorphoses and the poem is finally and simply the process of the image's life-history. Here is a poem called 'Centaurs' which clearly shows this process in action. It is as if the centaur notion is the larva from which the butterfly gorgeousness of the poem's movement emerges naturally:

I can think of William of Orange,
Prince of gasworks-wall and gable-end.
A plodding, snow-white charger
On the green, grassy slopes of the Boyne,
The milk-cart swimming against the current

Of our own backstreet. Hernan Cortes
Is mustering his cavalcade on the pavement,
Lifting his shield like the lid of a garbage-can.
His eyes are fixed on a river of Aztec silver,
He whinnies and paws the earth

For our amazement. And Saul of Tarsus,
The stone he picked up once has grown into a hoof.
He slings the saddle-bags over his haunches,
Lengthening his reins, loosening his girth,
To thunder down the long road to Damascus.

I think the wrong question here is 'What's it about?', the wrong quest the quest for the poem's relationship to the world outside it. Fundamentally, the poem displays the imagination's confidence and pleasure in re-ordering the facts of place and time, of history and myth. The milkman in the milkcart heading into a backstreet under the figure of William of Orange flourishes and blooms into voluptuous conceptions of Cortez and Saul of Tarsus. If we miss the opulence of the music, the overspill of the creative joy, we miss the poem. The life of the thing is in the language's potential for generating new meanings out of itself, and it is this sense of buoyancy, this delight in the trickery and lechery that words are capable of, that is the distinguishing mark of the volume as a whole.

I think this is where reviewers of Muldoon's earlier book missed the point when, after praising the technique, they asked what he had to say. What he has to say is constantly in disguise, and what is disguised is some conviction like this: the imagination is arbitrary and contrary, it delights in its own fictions and has a right to them; or we might quote Wallace Stevens: 'Poetry creates a fictitious existence on an exquisite plane.' In Muldoon, the plane varies from sequences like 'Armageddon, Armageddon', from a parable like 'Lunch with Pancho Villa' to a beautiful direct meditation like 'Paris'.

The hermetic tendency has its drawbacks, however, and leads him into puzzles rather than poems—at least, that's my response to some work here such as 'The Big House' and the 'Ducking Stool'; and when in different poems we find girls called Faith, Grace and Mercy, and a boy called Will, our patience with the mode gets near to breaking point. But it holds, finally, and gratefully, because most of the time, we know we can trust ourselves to Muldoon's good intentions. He is one of the very best.

Radio Telefís Eireann, 1978

213

Digging Deeper

Brian Friel's 'Volunteers'

'The great dramatic subject of internment deserves a great play': so the theatre critic of the *Sunday Independent* concluded his unsympathetic and symptomatic review of Brian Friel's *Volunteers* which had its *première* in the Abbey Theatre in 1975. He had seen a desperate and ironic play about internees, but his language deflected him towards the grandiloquent abstraction. That phrase, 'the great dramatic subject of internment', is symptomatic of the pieties and patriotism implicit in another phrase, now heard less and less from Dublin but once almost *de rigueur* when speaking of the Catholic minority in Ulster, who were 'our people in the North'. Both symptomatic phrases have indeed their essential truth, but that truth is devalued when they are bandied in a context where internment and the North have become a spectator sport.

Of course, the title of Friel's play courts the stock response. Volunteers answer the call, rise to the self-sacrificing occasion and are noble in the cause, whether of Ireland or Ulster. The word has a sacral edge which blunts (nevertheless) to sancti-moniousness, and it is this potential sanctimoniousness that the play is intent on devastating. Misery and bravery can be ennobled from a distance—the armchair poets of the First World War are a good example—but one of the artistic impera-tives is to say the truth as exactly as possible. The message implicit in Friel's play is explicit in Wilfred Owen's 'Apologia Pro Poemate Meo': 'These men are worth your tears. You are not worth their merriment.'

Like Owen's soldiers, and still more like his miners, Friel's internees are dug in—on an archaeological site. For five months

214

they have been on daily parole to assist the excavation of a Viking site that is soon to be buried under a multi-storey hotel. They have volunteered for the job, have been ostracized by their fellow internees for their collaboration and on this last day of the dig they learn that they are to be violently punished, probably killed, by their comrades back in the cells. They are trapped between political, economic and social realities and received ideas: victims, which is another word that Friel is intent on pursuing into accuracy. They come in under the indifferent eye of a warder, work their stint under the supervision of a petty bourgeois foreman and go out under the shadow of violent death. What happens in between is a masque of anarchy.

The action—or, more precisely, the interaction—centres on Keeney, a man who has put an antic disposition on, for Viking Ireland, like Denmark, is a prison. He is a Hamlet who is gay, not with tragic Yeatsian joy but as a means of deploying and maintaining his anger.

Volunteers to a large extent depends on the various plays within the play initiated by, directed by and starring Keeney, a shower-off and a letter-down, who uses as a starting-point for much of his improvisation the skeleton of a murdered Viking, exposed *in situ*, a bony structure that can be fleshed with any number of possible meanings: a symbol, in fact, as is the thirteenth-century jug lovingly restored by the site foreman.

A number of reviewers simply refused to accept the dramatic kind that Friel has broken into, a kind that involves an alienation effect but eschews didactic address. As a playwright he has always been obsessed by the conflict between public and private selves, by games and disguises. In *Philadelphia Here I Come*, he split his main character into two characters, Public and Private Gar O'Donnell, and vivified the perennial Irish father and son drama by this experimental, comic and enabling stroke. Double-talk and double-takes, time-shifts, supple dialogue and subtle exposures, these have been the life of his plays, but one occasionally sensed a tension between the vision and the form, as if a man whose proper idiom was free verse was being forced to realize himself in metrical stanzas.

In *Volunteers* he has found a form that allows his gifts a freer expression. Behind the writing there is an unrelenting despair at what man has made of man, but its expression from moment to moment on the stage is by turns ironic, vicious, farcical, pathetic. Friel would assent to the Yeatsian proposition that 'we traffic in mockery', although behind the mercurial histrionics of Keeney (marvellously played by Donal Donnelly) there looms the older saw that death is not mocked. The play is not a quarrel with others but a vehicle for Friel's quarrel with himself, between his heart and his head, to put it at its simplest. It is more about values and attitudes within the Irish psyche than it is about the rights and wrongs of the political situation, and represents a further digging of the site cleared in his *Freedom of the City*.

Still people yearn for a *reductio*: what does he mean? He means, one presumes, to shock. He means that an expert, hurt and shocking laughter is the only adequate response to a calloused condition (perhaps one should adduce Sassoon instead of Owen) and that no 'fake concern' (the phrase is the *Honest Ulstermans'*) should be allowed to mask us from the facts of creeping indifference, degradation and violence. And he means to develop as a playwright and to create, despite resistance, the taste by which he is to be enjoyed.

The Times Literary Supplement, 1975

Faith, Hope and Poetry

Osip Mandelstam*

'Art for art's sake' has become a gibe because of an inadequate notion of what art can encompass, and is usually bandied by people who are philistines anyhow. Art has a religious, a binding force, for the artist. Language is the poet's faith and the faith of his fathers and in order to go his own way and do his proper work in an agnostic time, he has to bring that faith to the point of arrogance and triumphalism. Poetry may indeed be a lost cause—like Jacobitism, as a young Scottish poet observed recently—but each poet must raise his voice like a pretender's flag. Whether the world falls into the hands of the security forces or the fat-necked speculators, he must get in under his phalanx of words and start resisting.

All this is made sure by the example of Osip Mandelstam, the Lazarus of modern Russian poetry. Mandelstam's last published book came out in 1928 and in 1938 he died in transit to one of Stalin's prison camps, aged forty-seven. In the meantime and for two decades after his disappearance, his name was almost totally erased from Soviet literary records. His books were confiscated, he became a 'non-person', and the poems of his last ten years were buried in three school exercise books which his widow carried through war and persecution like the ashes of an ancestor. Yet nowadays if an edition of his work were to be published in Russia it would sell out in minutes. Mandelstam's faith, it would seem, has been justified:

> The people need poetry that will be their own secret
> to keep them awake forever,

* Osip Mandelstam, *Selected Poems*, translated by Clarence Brown and W. S. Merwin, O.U.P., 1973; Clarence Brown, *Mandelstam*, C.U.P., 1973.

217

and bathe them in the bright-haired wave
of its breathing.

Mandelstam served the people by serving their language. His
early poems were written in association with the Acmeist poets,
a group whose ideas parallel those of the Imagists and who came
together at almost the same time. These first poems are fastidi-
ous and formal, breathing the air of the whole European literary
tradition, exhaling themselves back into that air as a tang of
Russian; yet one can see the organic link between the Parnassian cool of these lines, written in 1915:

> This day yawn like a caesura: a lull
> beginning in the morning, difficult, going on and on:
> the grazing oxen, the golden languor powerless
> to call out of the reed the riches of one whole note,

and the bare authority of this, written in exile twenty years
later:

> When my string's tuned tight as Igor's Song,
> when I get my breath back, you can hear
> in my voice the earth, my last weapon,
> the dry dampness of acres of black earth.

And in another poem to that black Russian soil he asks it to be
'the dark speech of silence labouring'. As Clarence Brown puts
it, Mandelstam was an aural poet: 'He heard his lines and took
them down, having wrested them from silence, from what he
could not, at first, hear.' Everything—the Russian earth, the
European literary tradition, the Stalin terror—had to cohere in
an act of the poetic voice; 'So Ovid with his waning love/wove
Rome with snow in his lines'—this voice of poetry was absolute
for him.

Mandelstam obliterates the Yeatsian 'choice' between perfection of the life or of the work. In 1971 he entered the martyr-
ology of Russian literature when his widow's memoir, *Hope
against Hope*, was published in the West. That story began with
Mandelstam's arrest because of a poem he had written against
Stalin. It had not been published, but an informer's whisper
was enough to lead to his three-year exile in Voronezh
(1934–37) and his second arrest and death, from heart-failure,
almost immediately afterwards.

218

Still, if Nadezhda Mandelstam is one of the great sustaining muses of our time, inspiring and literally carrying the poems from silence into the world, Clarence Brown is one of the best advocates that any poet has ever found. His book covers Mandelstam's early life and work, up until the end of the twenties, and is the result of almost twenty years' immersion in the poetry and research into the life. As a biographer and critic, Clarence Brown works with a double sensitivity: he gets inside his subject to comprehend, to feel with him and affect the reader; but he also stands outside to see the poet in a context and to test the poems against his extremely literate ear and cultivated common sense. The pace of his book is slow but not leisurely; the tone one of concern, of intimate involvement. He is Horatio to Mandelstam's Hamlet in the strict arrest of death, and the best compliment I can pay the book is to say that it measures up its dedication, which is to Nadezhda Mandelstam.

Clarence Brown also writes about the poems with beautiful insight into their techniques and linguistic texture, and with obvious gratitude and joy in their very existence. I cursed my ignorance of Russian as I followed his commentaries and as I read the versions of the poetry which he and W. S. Merwin have collaborated upon. *Selected Poems* contains work from all periods of Mandelstam's career, from the Acmeist verse of *Stone* to the last poems in exile, tears of fire and ice. The versions have the drift of contemporary American verse about them, and I have a notion that Merwin's rhythms soften the sculptured sounds of the Russian—inevitable, anyhow, when metrical, rhymed stanzas become free verse—but they nevertheless preserve the richness and uniqueness of Mandelstam's imagination, his premonition and almost celebration of doom and resurrection:

> Mounds of human heads are wandering into the distance.
> I dwindle among them. Nobody sees me. But in books
> much lived, and in children's games I shall rise
> from the dead to say the sun is shining.

We live here in critical times ourselves, when the idea of poetry as an art is in danger of being overshadowed by a quest for poetry as a diagram of political attitudes. Some commentators have all the fussy literalism of an official from the ministry of

219

truth. Mandelstam's life and work are salutary and exemplary: if a poet must turn his resistance into an offensive, he should go for a kill and be prepared, in his life and with his work, for the consequences.

Hibernia, 1974

Full Face

Robert Lowell*

The power and scope of poetry depend upon individual poets, what they are prepared to expect from it and how they are prepared to let it happen or to make it happen in their lives. Robert Lowell was exemplary in his dedication and achievement, and if there was some disagreement and some disappointment among his readers about the direction his gift took in *Notebook* and its progeny, there was never any doubt about the integrity and passion with which he pursued his artistic ambitions. There was a nineteenth-century sturdiness about the career. He was a master, obstinate and conservative in his belief in the creative spirit, yet contrary and disruptive in his fidelity to his personal intuitions and experiences.

There was a stylistic drama being played out all through his work. There was perhaps a conflict between his love of literature and his sense of his times, between his predilection for the high rhetorical modes of poetry and the age's preference for the democratic and the demotic. When, for example, I talked to him about that last buoyant poem in *The Dolphin*, the one beginning 'My dolphin, you only guide me by surprise', he said, in a self-deprecatory way, 'Oh, set-piece, set-piece', as if its self-contained energy, its finish and lift-off, were old hat. He did not really believe that, I think, but at that moment he was standing up for life against art, implicitly defending the bulk and flux of the less finished work that constituted the whole sequence.

That fourteen-line stanza or blank sonnet which he used compulsively during the years after *Near the Ocean* was an attempt

* Robert Lowell, *Day by Day*, Faber, 1978.

to get nearer the quick of life, to cage the minute. Yet Lowell was not essentially a poet of the present tense: he was a looker before and after, a maker, a plotter, closer to Ben Jonson than to D. H. Lawrence. The annotations of *Notebook* were always straining away from the speed and particularity of their occasions and pining for the condition of meditation. Was there a 'misalliance'—a word he uses forcefully in *Day by Day*—between the gift and the work it was harnessed to do? One is reluctant to say yes in face of the gigantic effort, the pile-up of magnificent things he brought off within the general plan, the honesty and daring with which he lived through private and public trauma in the late sixties and early seventies, and the boldness with which he wrote them out—but finally and reluctantly, yes is the answer.

One is all the surer of this on reading the best poems in *Day by Day*. Here he abandoned the arbitrary fourteen-line template to which he had been cutting his poetic cloth; the poems are in a variety of verse paragraphs and stanza forms, freed but not footless, following the movement of the voice, sometimes speaking formally, often intimately, occasionally garrulously. But the reader is kept in the company of flesh and blood. We are always being told something interesting or sorrowful even when the manner of the telling falls short of whatever we recognize to be his level best.

Day by Day might have been subtitled 'love songs in age', although this would not cover some of the more agonizing personal pieces, such as 'Visitors'—they arrived to take him to the mental institution: 'Where you are going, Professor, you won't need your Dante'—or the unrelenting poem about his mother called 'Unwanted', or the poem about his school days, 'St. Mark's, 1933', which has the coarse strength of a graffito. These and other poems crowd the book with specific autobiographical cries, yet I believe that the definitive poems are ones that conduct all his turbulence and love into a fiction or along the suggestions of an image—'Ulysses and Circe', for example, or the marvellous poem centred on Van Eyck's portrait of the Arnolfini Marriage and entitled simply 'Marriage':

> They are rivals in homeliness and love;
> her hand lies like china in his,
> her other hand

is in touch with the head of her unborn child.
They wait and pray,
as if the airs of heaven
that blew on them when they married
were now a common visitation,
not a miracle of lighting
for the photographer's sacramental instant.

There is a received literary language shimmering behind that writing and its simplicity and amplitude recall Pound's dictum that the natural object is always the adequate symbol. The feeling, being a bloom off the things presented, does not have to be stated, or restated. Lowell here attains what he calls in 'Epilogue', another of the book's definitive poems, 'the grace of accuracy':

Pray for the grace of accuracy
Vermeer gave to the sun's illumination
stealing like the tide across a map
to his girl solid with yearning.
We are poor passing facts
warned by that to give
each figure in the photograph
his living name.

The intimation of mortality in that last cadence is typical of many other moments in the book when a sad, half-resigned autumnal note enters and nowhere with more typical riddling force than in the poem for his son Sheridan:

Past fifty, we learn with surprise and a sense
of suicidal absolution
that what we intended and failed
could never have happened—
and must be done better.

Lowell's bravery was different from the bravery of John Berryman or Sylvia Plath, with whom his name has often been joined. They swam away powerfully into the dark swirls of the unconscious and the drift towards death, but Lowell resisted that, held fast to conscience and pushed deliberately towards self-mastery. His death makes us read this book with a new tenderness towards the fulfilments and sufferings of the life that lies behind it and with renewed gratitude for the art that he could not and would not separate from that life. It is not as braced and profiled as, say, *Life Studies*; rather the profile has turned to us, full face, close, kindly, anxious, testing—a husband's face, a father's, a child's, a patient's, above all a poet's.

Irish Times, 1978

Selected Bibliography

Clarence Brown. *Mandelstam.* New York: Cambridge University Press, 1973.

Clarence Brown and W. S. Merwin, trans. *Selected Poems of Osip Mandelstam.* New York: Atheneum Publishers, 1974.

Lord Dunsany. *The Charwoman's Shadow.* New York: Ballantine Books, Inc., 1977.

———. *Gods, Men & Ghosts: The Best Supernatural Fiction of Lord Dunsany,* Edited by E. F. Bleiler. New York: Dover Publications, Inc., 1971.

Geoffrey Hill. *King Log: Poems.* Chester Springs, Penn.: Dufour Editions, Inc., 1968.

———. *Somewhere Is Such a Kingdom: Poems, 1952–1971.* Boston: Houghton Mifflin Company, 1975.

———. *Tenebrae.* Boston: Houghton Mifflin Company, 1979.

Ted Hughes. *Crow: From the Life and Songs of the Crow.* New York: Harper & Row Publishers, Inc., 1971.

———. *The Hawk in the Rain.* London: Faber and Faber, Ltd., 1968. Distributed by Merrimack Book Service, Inc., Salem, N.H.

———. *Lupercal.* London: Faber and Faber, Ltd., 1960. Distributed by Merrimack Book Service, Inc., Salem, N.H.

———. *Wodwo.* New York: Harper & Row Publishers, Inc., 1967.

Patrick Kavanagh. *Collected Poems.* W. W. Norton & Co., Inc., 1973.

———. *Come Dance with Kitty Stobling.* Chester Springs, Penn.: Dufour Editions, Inc., 1964.

———. *The Great Hunger.* Dublin: Cuala Press, 1971. Distributed by Biblio Distribution Centre, Totowa, N.J.

———. *Self Portrait: An Autobiographical Discourse* (2nd edition). Atlantic Highlands, N.J.: Humanities Press, Inc., 1975.

———. *Tarry Flynn.* Old Greenwich, Conn.: The Devin-Adair Co., Inc., 1949. See also Alan Warner.

Philip Larkin. *A Girl in Winter*. New York: The Overlook Press, 1976.

——. *High Windows*. New York: Farrar, Straus & Giroux, Inc., 1974.

——. *Jill*. New York: The Overlook Press, 1976.

——. *The North Ship*. London: Faber and Faber, Ltd., 1974. Distributed by Merrimack Book Service, Inc., Salem, N.H.

——. *The Whitsun Weddings*. London: Faber and Faber, Ltd., 1964. Distributed by Merrimack Book Service, Inc., Salem, N.H.

Michael Longley. *No Continuing City, Poems Nineteen-Sixty-Three-Nineteen-Sixty-Eight*. Chester Springs, Penn.: Dufour Editions, Inc., 1970.

Robert Lowell. *Day by Day*. New York: Farrar, Straus & Giroux, Inc., 1977.

The Hugh MacDiarmid Anthology: Poems in Scots and English. Michael Grieve & Alexander Scott, eds. Boston: Routledge & Kegan Paul, Ltd., 1972.

John Montague. *Chosen Light*. Chicago: The Swallow Press, Inc., 1970.

——. *The Great Cloak*. Winston-Salem, N.C.: Wake Forest University Press, 1978.

——. *The Rough Field* (revised edition). Winston-Salem, N.C.: Wake Forest University Press, 1979.

——. *A Slow Dance*. Winston-Salem, N.C.: Wake Forest University Press, 1975.

——. *Tides*. Chicago: The Swallow Press, 1971.

Paul Muldoon. *Mules*. Winston-Salem, N.C.: Wake Forest University Press, 1977.

Theodore Roethke. *Collected Poems*. New York: Doubleday & Co., Inc., 1975.

Stevie Smith. *Collected Poems*. New York: Oxford University Press, 1976.

Alan Warner. *Clay Is the Word: Patrick Kavanagh 1904–1967*. Atlantic Highlands, N.J.: Dolmen Press, 1974.